ACCORDING TO DORA

ACCORDING
TO DORA

DORA BRYAN
in association with Kay Hunter

THE BODLEY HEAD
LONDON

British Library Cataloguing
in Publication Data

Bryan, Dora
According to Dora.
1. Bryan, Dora   2. Actors — Great Britain
— Biography
I. Title   II. Hunter, Kay
792'.028'0924   PN2598.B73/

ISBN 0 370 31030 6

Printed in Great Britain for
The Bodley Head Ltd
32 Bedford Square, London WC1B 3EL
by Butler & Tanner Ltd
Frome and London
set in Linotron Palatino
by Falcon Graphic Art Ltd
Wallington, Surrey

First published 1987

LIST OF PLATES

ACKNOWLEDGEMENTS

Thanks are due to Chappell Music Limited for permission to publish an extract from the song 'Why did you call me Lily?' on page 81.

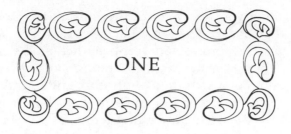

ONE

I WAS IN MY DRESSING ROOM AT THE NATIONAL THEATRE in London. It was at the end of my fiftieth year in show business. To pass the time between entrances I tried to remember all the dressing rooms I had been in during those years.

The room at the National was very businesslike; strictly utilitarian with no frills, and I can remember livelier dressing rooms. I once shared with a magician and his coloured doves. A few coloured doves might have helped in that dressing room on the South Bank, because I did feel rather isolated. The trouble was that I daren't leave it to look for companionship — I was so terrified that I might get lost in that maze of National Theatre corridors and miss my cue, as other artists have been known to do. So, apart from the intervals, when I escaped for coffee with my friends, I sat there between entrances doing tapestry, or listening to the radio on the built-in speaker. One could also listen in to the plays being rehearsed from the stages of the three theatres forming the National Theatre — the Olivier, the Cottesloe, or the Lyttelton, where our own play *She Stoops To Conquer* was in performance.

1

It's a long way and a lot of dressing rooms between that and the Palace Theatre, Manchester, in 1935, when I made my first professional appearance at the age of twelve. There was no chance of being lonely then, as I shared the room with the twenty-three other little girls who formed the Eileen Rogan Drury Lane Babes. I don't know why we went under that name, as we certainly never appeared at Drury Lane. I did so many years later, but that's another story. My first appearance was in *Jack and the Beanstalk*, and I was singled out to do some sketches with the two comedians, G.S. Melvin and Billy Daniels. The role of Mrs Hardcastle in *She Stoops To Conquer* is a far cry from that, and from the little girl Dora May Broadbent from Oldham.

Although I was born in Parbold, Lancashire, I always think of myself as an Oldham girl, and I did spend four years with Oldham Repertory Company in those early days. But it was not until 1966 that the well-drilled, fast-tapping Drury Lane Babe of the 1930s actually played at London's Drury Lane Theatre. I took over from Mary Martin in *Hello, Dolly!*, and played it for two years. I was in illustrious company. Dolly had been played in America by such stars as Carol Channing, Eve Arden, Ginger Rogers, Betty Grable, Martha Raye, and Pearl Bailey in the all-black cast. It was also played by Carole Cook in Australia and Annie Cordy in Paris. My salary was £500 a week. Rumour had it that Mary Martin took ten times that amount, but I was thrilled to do it after being asked at a smart lunch with Hugh ('Binkie') Beaumont of the H.M. Tennent Organization, and the American producer David Merrick. I was so over the moon that I rushed down Regent Street to Liberty's and bought my husband two cashmere sweaters, and a Bonnie Cashin coat for myself. Then on to the Ladybird Shop for children's clothes . . . I felt exactly the same kind of thrill in the summer of 1985, when I was asked to play at the National Theatre. But Bonnie Cashin has closed, the Ladybird Shop isn't there any more, the children are in their twenties, and Bill has enough sweaters.

I was reminded of *Hello, Dolly!* when I sang 'Before the Parade Passes By', a song from the show. It was for a television performance from the Palace Theatre. Princess Anne was Guest of Honour, and after the presentation a brigadier said to me, 'Miss Bryan, you're a comedy lady. Your song didn't make us laugh.' It wasn't meant to. The song was about wanting to get back to really living again, after being a widow for some years. Oh well, you can't please everybody. Comedian Frank Carson cheered me up by whispering one of his inimitable 'one-liners' in my ear. As we applauded Princess Anne on her way out, Frank said, 'I didn't see her act. Was she any good?'

I do miss the comics when I work in the 'legitimate' theatre. I miss the band calls and the dancers, so it was lovely to be back in pantomime at the end of 1985, in *Aladdin* at Brighton; among the tap shoes, the sequins and feathers, and all the panto paraphernalia which launched me into show business when I was just a little girl.

As far back as I remember we lived in the Garden Suburb in Oldham. I had a very happy childhood. Mum was a farmer's daughter from Coppull, near Chorley, and Dad was a director of a small cotton bobbin mill, travelling the north of England in his Baby Austin, known as 'Emma'. I had a blond handsome brother, John, three years older than I was. I idolized John, and used to follow him around like a faithful little dog. Sometimes when Dad visited a nearby mill on business he would take me with him, and while he was in the mill I would sit happily in the car, rummaging through his big suitcase of samples, playing with the bobbins. Or I would sit by the streams which usually ran by the mills, and watch all the colours of the dyes. No one in our family had the remotest connection with the theatre, nor had they any desire to appear before the public, unless you count Aunt Minnie, who sang and played the piano at Christmas and birthday parties.

My first twelve years were fairly uneventful. Although we weren't poor in the strict sense of the word, we didn't have a lot of money. Mum always did all the decorating herself, and we were always well dressed and much loved. I even had a pair of ice skates, and my brother John was the owner of a bicycle, which was quite something. Mum made most of my clothes, and rarely did I have an off-the-peg dress. I remember what a treat it was to go on the bus with Mum and buy one from Lewis's in Manchester — I did once squeeze into a Shirley Temple style dress. I suppose it was from my mother that I inherited my energy. She also had a wonderful sense of humour. She could start to tell a funny story and have me laughing helplessly long before she reached the end.

Our treats were simple enough. We would go to Blackpool, bouncing along in 'Emma', leaning out of the windows as we competed for the penny Dad had promised to the first of us to spot Blackpool Tower in the distance. Then there was my favourite outing — a matinée in Manchester, holding on to the edge of the gallery seat at what seemed a dizzy height from the stage. The first show I ever saw was *Peter Pan*, and I longed to be Peter, just as I came away from an ice-skating film with visions of being another Sonja Henie. After seeing Ingrid Bergman in *Intermezzo* I had a Swedish accent for days, until my brother told me to stop talking silly.

The Garden Suburb was an ideal place for children to

4

try out their talents. It was a friendly, sociable place, where there was always something going on for all ages: whist drives, parties, dances, charity concerts, and all manner of activities. The big annual event was the ceremony of the Rose Queen, which took place in June. John and I used to look forward to the fancy dress parade. One year we went as Mickey and Minnie Mouse, and another year as the Bisto Kids. When the Rose Queen rode in her procession through the streets, I would invariably be trotting behind in the role of a petal thrower, but later, when I was old enough, I was elected as the Rose Queen herself. I wore a beautiful satin dress with a six-foot pink and white train, with pink and white satin roses on it, handmade by Mum, as was the whole outfit. The day I was crowned in front of the entire population of the Garden Suburb was the day I had my first taste of stage fright. My knees shook uncontrollably.

I always loved to dance, so Mum took me along to Miss Eileen McNeill's dancing school in Oldham, where I soon became what's known as 'a leading light'. At one of the end of term concerts I delighted everyone with my rendering of 'There's Something About A Soldier', clad in full guardsman's uniform. Then there was 'Tiptoe Through The Tulips', which was all a bit strange, because for some reason I performed it while dressed as a daffodil! No matter. I had some nice notices in the local papers such as 'That's what she's cut out for ...', 'Dancing with a thrill in it ...', and 'Ten-year-old Dora Broadbent captivated everyone with the musical number "Roll up the carpet; Get some music on the radio". A dancer with personality; a real comedienne.'

I enjoyed every minute of my dancing lessons, and after two years with Miss McNeill, she suggested to Mum that I really ought to be given a stage training. A school was chosen for me in Manchester, run by Eileen Rogan and her husband Frank Gordon, who had been Gertrude Lawrence's first husband. Not that I even knew at that time who Gertrude Lawrence was, but Mum seemed terribly impressed by this little snippet of information. That was the beginning of my real training for the stage as a dancer, and it occupied three nights a week, from 6 p.m. to 8.30 p.m. My schooling became very erratic, but somehow I managed to win a scholarship to Oldham High School. The thought of leaving Hathershaw Council School and my lovely understanding headmaster, Mr Jones, was all too much for me. Who else would let me finish school at three-thirty, so I could catch the bus to Manchester, then another to Fallowfield, to get to dancing school in time for my lessons? Who else, later on, would have let me have time off school to go to London and Glasgow to appear in pantomime? With very little persuasion from me, Mum and Dad said I need not take up my scholarship — which at that time was the equivalent of the Eleven Plus — and I happily carried on at Hathershaw Council School.

There was one false start right at the beginning of my theatrical career. I was accepted for a Julian Wylie pantomime, but then it was discovered that I was five weeks too young. Children had to be twelve years old, and I just missed being the right age, so was bitterly disappointed. The next year my age was no problem, and I was chosen again by Julian Wylie, who picked me out at the dancing school to be one of the twenty-four Drury Lane Babes at the Manchester Palace. It was a great day for me when I joined the prim crocodile of Eileen Rogan's Babes, whom I had seen and envied as they walked through Manchester, dressed in their uniforms of navy blue reefer coats, blue hats, and black patent leather shoes with ankle-straps. We were terrible snobs! To us, the other juvenile troupe working in the city at that time were all rather common. They wore red coats, shoes and hats, and actually had *dyed* blonde hair, which at that time seemed pretty shocking. It was 1935, and very different from 1985, when nobody thought twice about hair being dyed at all, whether it was blonde, black, or bright green.

I was paid 2s.6d. a week because I was chosen to do the sketches with the two comedians, and that just about covered my bus fares. For a young lady of twelve, the routine throughout the run of *Jack and the Beanstalk* was quite strenuous. I would go to school in Oldham in the mornings, leave early to catch the bus to Manchester, have my lunch at the local UCP café, then go off to the theatre for the matinée. After the matinée, in order to satisfy the Education Authority, we had to have our lessons at the theatre. Our teacher, a dear lady, was far more interested in seeing that we had enough rest, so we were all taught how to relax. This was done by switching off all the lights in the dressing room, and lying on the floor in a row. Then the relaxation would start — first the toes, then the ankles, up to the knees, and so on until we reached our heads, by which time most of us were sound asleep, and so was the teacher. When the call-boy came to call 'Half an hour, please!' he would be greeted by a chorus of gentle snores from twenty-four sleeping Babes and one elderly teacher.

When I left home the following year to do a pantomime in Glasgow, we had to attend a school in the mornings, near to our digs, which were in a basement in Hill Street. We felt very isolated among all those strange children, who spoke quite differently from us. The teachers treated us as a temporary nuisance which had to be endured, and more or less ignored us. We were simply given a desk and a book each, and as long as we kept quiet we were left to our own devices. It was a very large class, so the less the teacher had to do with us, the better it was, from her point of view. I spent most of my time writing long letters to Mum, and keeping a diary. Apart from being desperately home-sick, it was my misfortune during the run of that pantomime to be Matron's Pet. This is an awful experi-ence, and a dreaded situation for any red-blooded juvenile. It meant sleeping in the same room as Matron, or 'Auntie', as we were invited to call the poor woman put in charge of us as chaperone and surrogate mother while we were away from home. All right, it had a few 'perks', and you had butter instead of margarine, but there were enormous disadvantages as well. There were no midnight feasts with the other girls, and no long talks in bed at the end of the day. I felt very left out of things, and the girls were frightened to include me in the bits of gossip in case I passed them on to Matron.

It's strange how small things can upset us when we are children, and minor incidents can blow up into major issues which can ruin a whole day. I always dreaded Saturday matinées during that Glasgow panto-mime because I was worried the whole afternoon about which of the Glasgow football teams — Celtic or Rangers — had won their matches that day. Now that may sound very strange, but it really was vital, because in the Finale of the show, my friend Vera Swindells and I came on stage dressed as representatives of the respective teams, wearing shorts and striped shirts in the appropriate colours. I was chosen to represent Rangers, and as far as I can remember my colours were royal blue, white and black. On Saturday nights we would walk downstage in turn in the Finale, and if Rangers had won their match that afternoon I would be cheered and given a box of chocolates. Vera received the same if Celtic won. If the teams lost, we were booed. I hated being booed, and took it very personally;

8

it was almost as though it was my fault that they'd lost, and that booing was really hurtful. It was enough to put me off football for ever, and I found myself wondering, all through the matinée, in a morbid sort of way, how Rangers had got on.

It was while I was in Glasgow for that pantomime season that one of the other girls in the group introduced me to the lucrative but terrifying business of shop-lifting. I would like to declare absolutely truthfully to Messrs Woolworth that I never had the nerve to indulge in this myself, but I used to follow my friend around while she filled her pockets with shampoo, toothpaste, hair nets, hair grips, and other useful toiletries, filched from the counters when no one was looking. She would then sell these items to the rest of us at a reduced price and make herself a nice little profit. I wasn't the slightest bit shocked at her behaviour, just filled with admiration at her courage, because I was such a coward.

The following year I was in *Mother Goose* at the London Hippodrome. This theatre later became Talk of the Town, but now I'm glad to say Peter Stringfellow has restored its original name. This was a real star-studded pantomime, with George Lacy as Mother Goose, Florence Desmond as principal boy, Chili Bouchier as principal girl, Max Wall, Mamie Souter, and — of all things — the famous classical dancers Alicia Markova and Anton Dolin as the speciality dancers. I don't think they were very happy in this particular engagement, and as we Babes waited in the wings, they would come off and grumble about the uneven stage, and they always looked in a thoroughly bad temper. But they were charming to us, and gave us all a tuppenny bar of chocolate every week.

Florence Desmond was my favourite. I suppose this was because she showed me what a star's home was like. She invited all the Babes home for tea one day, to her flat in St John's Wood — all twenty-four of us! After our theatrical digs in New Cross, this seemed like real living, and I wanted it to go on for ever. So this was what it was like to be a *star*, I thought. We had a marvellous tea, with a large cake, trifles and jellies, and we all came away with boxes of chocolates. Florence Desmond's husband, the famous flyer Charles Hughesdon was there too. He was later killed in a flying accident. He was very handsome, and I was saddened when, years later, I heard about his death. I remember to this day what Miss Desmond wore on the day of that tea party. It was a grey pleated skirt, grey cashmere sweater, and flat-heeled brogues. She looked just as gorgeous to me as she did in her principal boy's costume which she wore on stage. To a crowd of homesick children, a tea party at a lovely home, with the use of a glamorous bathroom, meant far more than all the expensive presents. Although I must say that nowadays the children I work with in pantomimes seem very laid back and sophisticated. Not like the Drury Lane Babes at all!

Another party was given for us under the stage one day, between the matinée and evening performances. All the principals came, and I think they enjoyed it just as much as we kids did, particularly when we did impersonations of them doing their numbers from the show. I remember I did my version of Mamie Souter, impersonating a little girl finding a worm under her skirt. I can't think that this could have been terribly amusing or clever, as I was such a little girl myself.

It was usual for children in pantomime to choose one of the chorus or show girls to be a kind of guardian angel and elder sister during the run of the show. They were known, perhaps unfortunately, as the 'Big Girls', and on the first day of rehearsal you gave the girls the once-over and decided which one you were going to ask to be your Big Girl. The tradition was that you were taken out to tea by them occasionally, you bought them presents and generally idolized them, and told them all your troubles. I was very lucky in choosing a really nice girl called Bonny. She had lovely blonde hair cut with a fringe, and she was head girl of her troupe. She would take me to a Lyons Corner House once a week after the matinée and buy me a lovely tea with a banana split to finish. Bonny was my Big Girl for two pantomimes, and corresponded with me for a long time afterwards. She even sent me clogs from Holland, and edelweiss from Switzerland when she was working there. I still have them, and often wonder if she realizes that the little homesick Dora Broadbent she once looked after is now someone called Dora Bryan.

I don't remember much about our digs at New Cross, except that they seemed an awfully long way from the theatre. After two shows each day, the journey back to New Cross at night seemed endless. I was fortunate to be able to spend most Sundays with my auntie and uncle who lived in Ilford, in Essex, and on Sundays I ate as much as I could, to make up for what I missed of home cooking during the week.

After that London pantomime I was fourteen years old, which meant that I was old enough to leave school. Miss Rogan sent six of us out on a variety tour, billed as the Gaiety Girls. We also did a summer season at Great Yarmouth in Walter Paskin's *Come to the Show* at the end of the pier. I enjoyed that. We had a pleasant matron as 'Auntie', and no one had to share her room because she liked to sleep alone. She fed us on Yarmouth bloaters and bread and margarine, which wasn't exactly exciting or imaginative fare, but as I loved bloaters — and still do — the diet suited me fine. We were paid only 7s.6d. a week for that show, because

11

Miss Rogan shrewdly pronounced that it was more like a holiday for us, and would build us up for the pantomime season! We all became very sun-tanned during that summer by the sea, and when not on the beach we spent our off-duty time at the cinema, where we were allowed in for nothing because we were 'pros'.

In the show we did a very strenuous high-kick routine to the accompaniment of the *Poet and Peasant* overture. We had xylophones strapped to our backs, and we turned around and played the melody on our partner's back in between a lot of high kicks. I can still feel the thuds of those xylophones on my spine! We would come off stage nearly fainting, and I used to think that there must be an easier way of earning a living. Then there was my speciality number with my friend Vera Swindells. It was to the music of 'Me and my Shadow', and we were dressed as boxers in black satin shorts and white satin blouses. There were bells strapped around our waists all tuned to the note of F, and more sets of bells around our wrists and ankles, which played other notes. We came on from the wings in a blackout, with just a spot on us, and singing 'Me and my Shadow' with little mirrors in our hands. Then we would single out someone in the audience, shine our mirrors on to the one so chosen, and sing to that one person. Everything seemed to be full of bits of apparatus. The finale of this number was a slow motion boxing match, while playing a shaky version of 'The Skaters' Waltz' on the bells which were strapped to the various parts of our anatomy. It was quite a performance! One year, in the *Night of a Hundred Stars*, the annual charity show at the London Palladium, I danced 'Me and my Shadow' with John Gilpin. It crossed my mind at the time what a difference there was between the celebrity-packed Palladium that night, and the theatre in Yarmouth all those years previously.

After that summer season Mum decided that although I was a 'dancer with personality', I wasn't going to get very far with the Drury Lane Babes — or even the Gaiety Girls for that matter. She also realized that I was only a competent dancer, and a lazy one at that, so it was decided that I would become an actress, even though I wasn't exactly burning with ambition in that direction. I was beginning to compare my life with the lives of my friends at home, and theirs seemed to be much more enjoyable. They were joining tennis clubs, acquiring boy friends, attending parties, and going to Pitman's College in Manchester to train as shorthand typists. There was no doubt, I thought, that they were all having a whale of a time. And there was I, working every night, dancing until I dropped, with bells and xylophones stuck all over me. But Mum had made up her mind that although the dancing side might have to recede into the background, I was certainly not going to finish up as a shorthand typist. She decided to send me to a drama school in Manchester. I didn't mind too much, as I thought it was the next best thing to going to Pitman's. I was able to catch the same bus as my friends did in the mornings, and travelled home again with them at night. My social life was looking up.

A term at the drama school proved to be a complete waste of the eighteen-guinea fee. I didn't wish to know how to fence, or how to write a play. And as I already knew how to apply make-up quite successfully — I'd been doing it for years — there seemed to be little point in staying there any longer. My brief stay there, however, did enable me to enter, at the age of fifteen, for the Grade I examination in acting of the London Academy of Music. We had to go along to the Athenaeum in Manchester to take the exam, which consisted, among other things, of performing two scenes from plays — one Shakespeare scene and one from a modern play.

13

There were not just soliloquies, but each entrant had to speak the dialogue for two parts, becoming first one character and then the other. I was the youngest entrant, and survived the ordeal, discovering later that I had passed with honours. I still have the report, dated May 1939, from the Manchester Repertory Theatre School of Acting, which states:

> She is alert and obviously possesses a great sense of comedy. In fact, it is clear at this early stage that she is a born comedy actress. Her voice, however, needs considerable attention. It requires much more flexibility and a certain amount of polish, which no doubt she will acquire during her training. Her enunciation is very good.

I suppose the Manchester Repertory Theatre School of Acting anticipated that I was going to acquire all this polish during my training there, but I decided to leave before they had the chance to put the finishing touches to my elocution. Not that this sudden relinquishing of my training meant the end of my theatrical career by any means. Mum had the bit between her teeth, and she took me for an interview with the newly opened Oldham Repertory Theatre Club, which was based at that time in the Temperance Hall. I must have made a fairly good impression, because I was taken on as a student and assistant stage manager, all of which sounded much more interesting than the drama school. Because I was being admitted as a student, it was made clear that there would be no salary attached to the engagement, but somehow that didn't seem to matter too much.

Thus I embarked upon one of the happiest, most hardworking years of my professional life. Suddenly I knew, without a shadow of doubt, exactly where I was going and what I wanted to be: an actress. It must have

14

been some inbuilt juvenile self-preservation mechanism that made me decide never to mention my early days as a Drury Lane Babe. There seemed to me at the time to be a very firm dividing line between the legitimate side of the theatre and the 'illegitimate' aspect of variety, music hall and pantomime. I didn't want to appear to be any different from all the other members of the repertory company, with their London accents, and their sophisticated theatrical chat, peppered with the names of 'John', 'Noël', and 'Binkie'. (Who were they?) I was sure they would never have understood my prattle about Big Girls and Aunties, so I shut up and said nothing.

I was fifteen when I started at the Rep, and looked very young for my age. How lucky I was to be able to live at home with its comfort and security, after all those tatty theatrical digs. It was the best of both worlds, because when I had time I could still see my friends in the Garden Suburb, and not feel too different or cut off from them, as I had when I was a pantomime Babe. I don't think I have ever worked so hard or so uncomplainingly as I did at the Rep. Sundays were no different from any other working day, as I had to make the curtains and loose covers for the following week's production, and that had to be a Sunday job. Our producer would cut out the material and pin it all together, and I would take it home on the bus and try to make sense of it before the next day. Then there were props to be made, and the scenic artist always needed help with set painting, as weekly rep was a constant race against time.

The company soon became so popular that it was able to take over the Coliseum Theatre, eventually becoming known as one of the best reps in the country. If you'd worked at Oldham Rep, then you could say you'd had one of the best possible trainings, and it was a fine grounding for any aspiring teenager. We were very much pioneers when we moved to the Coliseum, and the amenities for actors and staff were fairly basic. There was just one dressing room for the women and one for the men, but in later years they acquired luxuries like showers and real bathrooms.

The title of Assistant Stage Manager — or ASM — in rep is a very misleading one. It may sound rather grand, but it really meant being willing to do absolutely anything — borrowing and begging props from family, friends, and local shopkeepers, sweeping the stage, painting sets, helping the stage hands, prompting, putting on 'effects' records for off-stage noises . . . there was no end to the work. The other student ASM with me was John Shuttleworth, and we were good friends. He was a very confident, good-looking, fair-haired boy with a lot of ambition. He now has his own theatre in Australia, called the John Edmund Theatre. He changed his name, as I was about to do.

The essential requirement for putting on 'effects' records is that they must go on at precisely the right second, to correspond with what is happening on stage. I once managed to put on a record for a non-pianist actor at the wrong time, and he found himself nowhere near the stage piano when it suddenly began to 'play'. He had to make a mad dash across to the piano to catch up with the action, and wasn't at all pleased with me for causing a laugh in the wrong place. The job of ASM was full of hazards of various kinds. Not least was the precarious system we had for dimming the lights. Bearing in mind that we were dealing with electricity, the lights were dimmed by slowly immersing two iron rods into two buckets of water. I still can't imagine how this worked, or even why I was not electrocuted, but I just did as I was told in those days, and never asked questions.

Being ASM also meant that one had to be capable of playing a small part one week, and a leading role the next, while still carrying on with the other odd jobs as well. Because I was very young and green, my leg was pulled unmercifully at first, and I was sent on some strange errands, such as being told to go to the iron-monger's for a glass hammer. It was quite a major undertaking each week to borrow the requisite props for the next production, and return all those which had been borrowed for the last one. From time to time there were some very strange props to locate and transport, such as a skeleton and wheel-chair for a production of *The Wind and the Rain*. I managed to borrow both from Oldham Infirmary, put the skeleton in the wheel-chair, and pushed it down Oldham High Street to the theatre, causing some very strange looks from passers-by. It wasn't a sight normally seen on a Monday morning in Oldham. My mother, who became well accustomed to my borrowing from all and sundry, was never sur-prised to come to the show on a Monday evening — which she always did — and see on stage her best cushions, a selection of family ornaments, hearth rug, tea service, or even her best hat being worn by the leading lady.

Of all the producers we had at the Rep, my favourite, and I think the best, was Douglas Emery, but he could be extremely stubborn about small details. I went home from rehearsal one day and said to Mum, 'I have to have a yellow dress for next week.'

'You haven't got a yellow one,' replied Mum. 'You'll have to wear that blue one. You haven't worn that for six weeks.'

'But Mum, it has to be yellow, Douglas says, because the line in the play is, "She looks like a little daffodil".'

Mum could also be stubborn, and her response to this was, 'Well, you tell Douglas the line will have to be

17

changed to "She looks like a little bluebell".'

But Douglas won in the end, and Mum had to make me a yellow dress. She made all my clothes for the shows, and I think I'm right to blow her trumpet by saying that I must have been the best dressed ASM-cum-juvenile in rep at that time. How she did it, when there was strict clothes rationing and coupons which had to be handed over in return for materials and clothing, I don't know, because she kept up her high standard even in wartime. She would come to dress rehearsals every Monday, and it didn't matter how busy I was with my props and odd jobs, or how nervous I was about my part, I would still have to try on my dresses while she levelled the hems and made the final touches.

Apart from the fact that he was a good producer, Douglas Emery was a very good friend to me, and once saved me from getting the sack. One of the business-men who was on the committee which ran the Rep wanted to get rid of Dora Broadbent because of her Hollinwood accent. Hollinwood was five miles out of Oldham, and perhaps the accent was too much like his own! He wanted to replace me with a sophisticated actress from London, but Douglas stood by me. 'If she goes, I go,' he told the committee. So I stayed, being given increasingly better parts, and becoming very popular with the audiences. Because I was a local girl I soon became known as 'Our Dora', and a mutual affection grew up between the audiences and myself. This became so much of a personal relationship that when I was playing Jane Eyre one week, and reached the scene in which Rochester proposed to me, a parti-san lady in the stalls called out, 'Don't, Dora! He's too old for you!' Perhaps she was right. During the war the male actors were either too old for National Service, or were invalids, which meant we sometimes had some

18

very odd-looking juvenile leads. One was so old that he wore a red wig, and when he kissed me his false teeth would move about. One night he came on with both sets missing. I was fascinated. As I queued for the bus with the faithful after the shows I was never left in any doubt about their reactions to my performance. They let me know in no uncertain terms. One week I played a gypsy girl, Nubi, in a black wig, in *The Squall*, and this involved me in a seduction scene. That evening the bus queue was positively hostile, and seethed with tuts and clucks, while sorrowful glances were cast in the direction of a very embarrassed teenage actress.

This spilling over of my stage roles into my personal life even intruded into my job of borrowing props. One day I went to borrow a few items from one of my regular sources, and the nice lady in question, who had always been most helpful and co-operative, was suddenly quite aggressive. Much to my surprise she greeted me with, 'I'm lending nowt more to t'Rep. Not when they encourage you to use bad language like in t'play last night. It's not nice coming from you, Dora.'

I can't remember what the 'bad language' was, but I'm sure it was something terribly mild compared with what can be heard in a theatre today without audiences turning a hair!

It was nice to be almost grown up, despite the concern that I was being corrupted by bad language, and one of my treats was to go for coffee with my dad. Everyone connected with the cotton industry in the managerial sector used to go on 'The Change' as the Royal Exchange in Manchester was known. It was like the Stock Exchange. There is now a wonderful theatre-in-the-round inside the Royal Exchange, but then it was purely for business, and women were not allowed inside. I used to meet Dad for coffee in the Kardomah Café in St Anne's Square. It was delicious; very sophisticated. We only drank Camp Coffee at home, which was the usual alternative to tea in most households at that time. Now everyone has grown accustomed to today's ground instant coffees, but the flavour of Camp Coffee, come to think of it, wasn't much like coffee at all. I do know that the Kardomah coffee tasted entirely different, and at fifteen years of age I felt that was just a start of splendid living. My sixteenth birthday was coming up, and Dad had a friend who had something to do with the diamond market. This was another of those great moments when life seemed to be opening up, because Dad's friend said I could choose a diamond for my birthday. Now there was something for a lass from the Garden Suburb.

Mum and Dad sat around while Dad's friend unfolded a silk handkerchief with slow deliberation. There inside was a selection of real diamonds in all different sizes. Much later in life I had to sing 'Diamonds are a Girl's Best Friend' in a musical, but on this occasion I wasn't worldly wise, and I thought the smallest diamond was the prettiest, so I chose that one. Mum and Dad were very disappointed that I didn't make better use of the opportunity, and their faces changed, their smiles of pleasure fading as their daughter made her fatal choice. But there was nothing they could say, of course, and I was quite happy with my tiny diamond, which soon got lost anyway.

After some considerable time at the Rep I began to be rather fed up with trying to do everything at once. It really was very hard work to play leads and fulfil all the duties of Assistant Stage Manager as well, but as I was by that time a very good and experienced ASM, nobody considered relieving me of the job. There is such a thing as being too efficient for one's own good. One of my friends in the company suggested that I should do a bit of slacking; forget the odd prop now and again. This went against the grain, but I must say that it did have some effect. I think the management finally got the message on the Monday we opened with a play for which the props list called for several bottles of milk. I decided to 'forget' the milk, but then had pangs of conscience and fear at the last minute. I was still something of a coward, and anyway I was rather proud of doing things properly. By the time my conscience had taken control again I had left it too late to buy the milk, so I did the next best thing, and filled the bottles with a mixture of white distemper and water, putting them in their rightful positions just before the curtain went up. They looked real enough, but unfortunately I had forgotten that one of the luckless actors had to drink some of the stuff during the course of the play.

You can't spend four years in a company without one or two unforeseen disasters, and certainly there were occasions when it wasn't necessary to make definite plans to be a nuisance. Things did have a habit of going wrong without a helping hand, as they did in a performance of *Saint Joan*. I was again doing several things at once, and in addition to being ASM I was playing a couple of walk-ons, as a page in one scene and a monk in another. The scene of Joan's trial is very long and wordy, and can be tedious if there's nothing to do but sit there without anything to say. I had solved the problem of this nightly boredom by passing my time as a silent monk with a bit of subversive knitting. I sat with my back to the audience, happily knitting away under my robes and working at a sweater, which was growing nicely. Unfortunately there came a night when an undersized monk shuffled reverently off the stage, head bowed, and trailing behind him a large and conspicuous ball of red Kwik-Knit wool.

We did Ibsen's *Ghosts* during the month of November. It was cold and foggy, and the audience was sparse. I think it must have been at the time I was fed up, and it was an evening when the producer had taken the night off to go to the Manchester Opera House. The interval music which had been chosen for *Ghosts* was something appropriately solemn, and it all added to the gloom and doom of Ibsen on an already miserable night. I'd just bought a lovely Joe Loss record of 'In the Mood', so I thought I would cheer everybody up during the interval. I put it on the turntable at full blast, and Mr Loss's foot-tapping rhythm blared out. I peeped through the curtain. The audience had perked up considerably. The second side of the record was 'The Woodchoppers Ball', which I'm sure would have done wonders for audience morale, but suddenly the producer, (who hadn't gone to Manchester after all, because of the fog), materialized from nowhere, absolutely furious. He smashed the record and threatened me with the sack, and I cried all the way home, partly because of his wrath, but I think mainly at the loss of my record, which had cost 4s.7½d. This was a major slice of my salary. Although I wasn't paid at all the first year, during the second year I received 7s.6d. a week. Despite my misdemeanours I eventually shed the irksome duties of ASM to become leading lady, when the salary crept up to twenty-five shillings. I was so happy! I gave Mum a pound, and had five shillings to spend on myself.

When the war came Oldham Rep carried on as usual, and so did I. We had our fire-watching duties to do one night a week, which meant spending the night in the theatre, keeping an eye open for bombs. We were also given a stirrup pump but no instructions on how to use it. There were compensations, as it was an opportunity to learn lines, and at least you were already there for the next day's rehearsals. The fire-watching drill was amazingly simple: if there was an air raid and an incendiary bomb should happen to come down in the theatre, you just shouted for the fireman to come and put it out, but I was never called upon to do this. If an air raid warning was in progress during a show the audience was not allowed to leave the theatre until the All Clear, so if they had to stay on after the play finished, we used to devise an impromptu entertainment for them. I was always in great demand for this as I had a repertoire of numbers left over from the days of the Drury Lane Babes. I'm sure everyone wondered where I'd learned them, but I never revealed my dark secret.

It was while we were giving one of these after-the-show concerts that I was 'discovered'. I didn't know it, but in the audience that night was a Mr Walker from the Variety Theatre, and after hearing my rendering of 'Me and my Shadow', he decided I was just the girl he wanted in his next pantomime to play Cinderella to the Prince Charming of Hannah Watts, in real life Countess Poulett. So the Rep very kindly gave me two months' leave to go off and play Cinders with Frank E. Franks, the Geordie comic, as Buttons. After playing for a month at the Variety Theatre at Oldham we did a four-week tour, and Mum came with me as 'Auntie'. It wasn't the large-scale pantomime I had been used to as a child, but at least we had some livestock on stage in the form of real ponies, which pulled Cinderella's coach. These were always borrowed in each town we played. I'm not quite sure what they did for the rest of the year, but they weren't very well trained theatrical ponies, and had a strange kind of fetish about my white pompadour wig. For my transformation scene from rags to the lovely silk ball gown with the white wig, my quick change would be laid out on a dust sheet in the wings. I had to pop out through the fireplace during the stage blackout, and rush round the back to do the quick change. The ponies invariably got to the white pompadour wig before I did, and in the blackout I could smell that things weren't quite as they should be with that wig. Never mind, the show must go on, so it was a case of giving the thing a vigorous shake and putting it on. When I think about it, Cinderella must have gone to the ball smelling rather peculiar.

All this went to my head in more ways than one. I was being paid the vastly increased salary of £8 a week as the pony-perfumed Cinderella, and at the end of the run it seemed a bit much to go back to my meagre Rep salary, even if it had been increased to £2 a week. Mum and I decided it was time to ask for more money, so between us we composed a letter to the Rep, broadly suggesting that it wasn't quite seemly for Cinderella to undergo a reversal of fate in the form of riches to rags. To this day I still have their reply:

January 24, 1941

Miss Dora Broadbent,
The Queen's Theatre,
South Shields

Dear Miss Broadbent,

In reply to your letter, which was read at the committee meeting last night, the committee are very pleased to offer you a re-engagement with this company at a salary of TWO POUNDS TEN SHILLINGS per week. [The capital letters are theirs, not mine.] This is an increase of TEN SHILLINGS per week on the salary you were receiving when you left us. Will you please let us know by return if you accept this offer, and when you will be at liberty to rehearse.

Sincerely yours
p.p. Oldham Repertory Theatre Club

So back I went to the Rep, none the worse for my

brief departure into the 'illegit' side of the theatre, and ten bob a week better off. I was doubly pleased to be home again, because just before signing the Cinderella contract, I had met Bill.

Our meeting was perhaps inevitable in a small town, but it can hardly be described as romantic. I was in the habit of walking half the way home from the Rep in the evening to save a penny on my bus fare, and one Friday night as I passed the public conveniences in the centre of the town there were four boys standing outside. Three of them gave a long low whistle as I walked past. I ignored them and, looking as disdainful as I could, I joined the queue at the bus stop. But there had been something interesting about the fourth boy, and as I waited I took a surreptitious glance at him. He was very tall and dark, with the nicest eyes. Very Gregory Peck, I thought, as I stepped on to my bus.

The following night was Saturday, and after the show I went to the Conservative Club dance with my brother. Oh dear, there was that tall dark boy again, and he was even better looking than I remembered. He was in the company of another blonde; not, I was gratified to note, a natural blonde like myself, but even so, she was still far too attractive for my liking.

For a while I made the best of things with my two good friends Arthur and Peter. Then Peter unwittingly did me a good turn for which I have been grateful ever since. He asked the unnatural blonde to dance, leaving the tall dark boy free to ask me, which he did. I was so overcome that I could hardly speak. He was equally shy, but managed to clear his throat and blurt, 'I saw you at the bus stop last night.' After I had shakily responded with the brilliant reply, 'Oh, did you?' we danced the rest of the quickstep in almost total silence. Just for once, Dora Broadbent, the chatterbox always full of confidence, was suddenly a bundle of nerves, but

25

my bumbling incoherence apparently did not put him off, because he came across and asked me for the next dance . . . and the next . . . and the next. I found out that his name was Bill Lawton. At the end of the evening came the last waltz, which was 'Who's Taking You Home Tonight?', and afterwards he asked me just that. My heart sank, seeing romance fly out of the window as I had the humiliation of replying, 'My brother.'

So I was walked home to Green Lane that night by Bill, but with my brother four paces behind. It was enough to blight the romantic feelings in any young man, but happily Bill wasn't easily blighted. I have to admit, however, that although I was sad when my ever loving and protective brother volunteered for the navy, my sadness was mixed with a kind of guilty relief that at least Bill and I would be able to spend some time alone.

Some boys would have been a little fed up about having a girl friend who worked every night, but it happened to suit Bill very well, because apart from working at Ferranti's in Hollinwood, making aircraft parts, he went to evening classes each night to study electrical engineering. The members of the Rep grew accustomed to seeing him hovering in the shadows outside the stage door as he waited for me. He could never be persuaded to come backstage. Our pleasures were very simple. Sometimes we would stop at the fish and chip shop on the way home. On Saturdays we went dancing, and on Sundays he came to our house, where he would hear me through my lines for the following night's new show. Bill played cricket, and our social life expanded to include the cricket club dances too. He eventually became a professional cricketer, and a very good one. He played in the Central Lancashire League, and in fact in all of the Northern Leagues. He also played for Lancashire against the Australians at Old Trafford.

My other boy friends remained 'just good friends', but Arthur didn't give up as easily as the others. He invited me to his house to tea one Sunday, and that all seemed harmless enough, especially as Bill was going cycling with some of his friends that day. After tea Arthur and I went for a walk to Daisy Nook, and to my horror, who should come cycling towards us but Bill! Because he was regarded as my 'steady' I had thought it was simpler not to mention my visit to Arthur's house. There was a concrete road block nearby, as there were on so many roads during the war, and with great presence of mind I hastily departed from Arthur's side and hid behind it, while he and Bill chatted about this and that for what seemed like an interminable length of time. I thought Bill hadn't seen me, and was amazed when he raised his voice and said, 'Come on, Dora! You have to get home to go through your lines for tomorrow.'

I crawled out from behind my road block, and ashamedly said goodbye to Arthur. I'm afraid that marked the end of our friendship, and of my pathetic attempts at two-timing.

Those Sunday night sessions with Bill hearing my lines must have sounded very funny, especially when we had incongruous situations such as Bill reading the part of Hedda Gabler to my Mrs Elvsted. He was not entirely inexperienced, and told me he did once appear in a Sunday School play as a butler. He was so nervous on the first night that he said all his lines at once, not giving anyone else the chance to speak. Then when he came off stage he could not be persuaded to go back! He has never been one to seek the theatrical limelight, although a few years ago he allowed himself to be interviewed with me on TV, much against his better

27

judgement. Just before transmission I was in the make-up chair, hoping he wouldn't run out of the building, and I heard the senior make-up girl say to her junior, 'Get Mr Lawton for make-up.' A few minutes later the young girl returned with a scarlet face. On being asked where Mr Lawton was she replied, 'He's just told me what I can do with my make-up!' I vowed that I would never again let this happen to him, let alone to me. I was so nervous for him on the programme that every time the interviewer asked him a question, I found myself answering it.

Towards the end of my years at Oldham Rep I was earning the top salary of £5 a week. This was all very nice, and things were beautifully cosy, but Mum thought it was high time I moved on to greater things. There was life beyond Oldham, so we went off to London and an appointment with Harry Hanson, who ran the famous provincial Court Players, with rep companies all over the country. He offered me a job at Peterborough at £8 a week, and while Peterborough could hardly be described as the theatrical Mecca, it did afford the temptation of another £3 a week, which had to be a step in the right direction. I decided to accept.

My last night at Oldham Rep was very sad. The committee presented me with a complete set of Shakespeare's works (still not read after all these years!), and I walked home with Bill for the last time. I was about to leave behind all this familiar, comfortable routine, and the homely warmth. I was desperately miserable, especially about leaving Bill, but my ever understanding Mum consoled me. 'Never mind, love,' she said. 'If you still feel this way about him when you're twenty-one, your dad and I will give you our blessing. Then perhaps they'll have you back at the Rep, and you can get married.' Little did I imagine then that, when we eventually married, I would be an established success in London, or that it was going to take nine years to come about.

I was to begin rehearsals on 18 October 1941 as Judy in Keith Winter's play *The Shining Hour*, and I had decided that the name of Dora Broadbent wasn't going to look good in lights. (Did I really think names went up in lights at Peterborough?) Anyway, a new name had to be found, but there were certain restrictions as to what it could be, because my lovely dad had already bought me a wardrobe trunk for my clothes, and had had the initials 'D.B.' stamped on it. That curbed the imagination a bit, but Mum and I were in the kitchen when we spotted a box of matches on the table, made by the famous firm of Bryant and May. As May was my middle name we decided my new name would be Dora May. 'What about the D.B. on the trunk?' asked Dad. It had to be a 'B', so it became Bryant. But when I arrived in Peterborough, far from putting my name in lights, they hadn't even got it right, and had announced their new juvenile lead as Dora Bryan. So Dora Bryan I became from that day.

Many years later, when I told Sir Laurence Olivier how I changed my name, he was fascinated. He had recently married Joan Plowright. 'Oh, what a pity you changed it,' he commented. 'Broadbent — what a lovely name! It's rather like Plowright.'

I hated Peterborough. It was a twice-nightly company, and my extra three pounds a week was hard earned, as I seemed to have the leading part every week in such sagas as *Peg o' My Heart, Jeannie, Lass o'Laughter*, etc. It was something of a compensation that I had very good digs for twenty-five bob a week, including meals, but I missed my home and Bill. We wrote to each other every single day, and met whenever we could, but I was desperately lonely. I made very few friends, as I didn't go into the pub after the show each night, as most of the others did. Apart from the fact that I didn't drink in those days, I was always extremely hungry at the end of the day, and wanted my supper, so I would return to my digs and eat, and write a long letter to Bill.

After Peterborough I appeared in various reps for Harry Hanson, including Westcliff-on-Sea and Tunbridge Wells. I was really happy at Westcliff, sharing a flat with two friends, Sarah and Valerie, and a delightful family of mice who would wait in the fireplace for their supper when we came home from the theatre each night. Harry Hanson was a kindly man, very round and pink, and he wore a wig. He was something of a legend in the theatre, and stories about him were rife at the time. I wasn't in the company when he was said to have come on stage at the end of a successful season to make his usual speech. The play was *Rebecca*, and as playgoers will know, Rebecca never appears at all. When Harry came on stage after the show, wearing his best blond wig, it was too much for at least one member of the audience who called out, 'My God! Here comes Rebecca!'

Because it was wartime I was called up to do my ENSA service or go into a factory. It was a strange option, and naturally I chose to do ENSA service. I wonder if any theatre people expressed a preference for the factory? We took a very unsuitable play around the camps to entertain the troops. Sarah and Valerie came with me, and it really was quite a nice change after weekly rep. After this tour Sarah had an offer to go to Colchester Rep, and as we were such good friends I applied to go too. Robert Digby, the manager, gave me an interview and a subsequent job. I then had to tell Harry Hanson that I wouldn't be returning to him, but was going to Colchester instead. He was very sad about it all. 'Miss Bryan,' he said, trying to be persuasive, 'if you stay with me I have plans to build you up into

30

another Elsie Henighan.' Now there was a temptation. Elsie, I may say, was leading lady on the pier at Hastings, and had been with Harry's companies for years and years.

Without wishing to hurt his feelings by saying that I didn't think my future lay on the Hastings pier, I explained to Harry that playing leading parts twice nightly was making me come out in boils, and it would only be one performance a night at Colchester, and anyway the Colchester Rep got notices in *The Stage*. So Harry and I parted company, but many years later I met him at a party in Brighton. He asked me what I was doing, in tones which suggested that I couldn't possibly have done anything worthwhile since I'd left the Court Players. 'I've just finished a run of *Gentlemen Prefer Blondes* at the Strand Theatre, but I'm not doing anything at the moment,' I said. My reply played beautifully into Harry's hands. Completely ignoring the fact that I was telling him I'd just finished a West End lead, he shook his head sadly. 'I told you,' he said with a deep sigh. 'If you'd stayed with me I could have built you up into — yes — into another Elsie Henighan.'

I wish I'd met Elsie. I believe she was excellent.

Accommodation in Colchester during the war was very difficult to come by, and I had a hard time finding somewhere to live. I opened in *Peg o' My Heart*, and the next morning set off to look for digs. After two hours of fruitless searching, and a lot of inquiries which led nowhere at all, I was convinced that I would be homeless for the entire length of my stay. I was so depressed that I went into a sweet shop with my sweet ration coupons to buy something to keep up my spirits and replenish my flagging energy. It was in this shop that I was greeted by the nicest face I'd seen in Colchester that morning. 'Faith if it isn't Peg herself!' exclaimed

31

the lady behind the counter in a lovely Irish brogue. 'It was grand to hear a bit of the old tongue at the Rep last night.'

My spirits rose rapidly. Here was a nice sympathetic lady, I thought, and went into my homeless-little-actress routine. 'I'm trying very hard to find digs,' I said, with what I hoped was the right touch of helplessness. 'Do you know of anyone who'd have me?'

'Well now,' she replied. 'I couldn't let another Irish-woman down. You can have my son's room here if you like. He's away. He's been called up.'

I waited until I was completely settled in before telling her that I came from Lancashire, but fortunately she didn't seem to mind at all. So there I was with digs in a sweet shop, which was an enviable place to be during wartime. But there weren't only sweets; there was homemade ice cream as well! I would be wakened each morning by the sound of the ice cream mixer churning away, and then came breakfast in bed, with stewed fruit and corn flakes, and a dollop of ice cream. What marvellous digs I had with my dear Auntie and Uncle Jeff, as I used to call them. They were so kind and hospitable. Auntie Jeff took a great interest in me, and in the theatrical way of life. She loved the whole scene, so much so that when I left another actress took over my room. Peggy Mount moved in, and I'm sure that the sweets and affection which had been lavished upon me were also afforded to Peggy when she took my place. I must admit that I had rather a reputation for being fond of my food. People would mention it as though it was some kind of unwholesome addiction. 'She's such a nice girl,' they would say to each other, 'but she *eats*.'

When I left Colchester after a few months, it was to do another tour of ENSA service. This time I went out with Colchester Rep as a company, and it was called 'Lease-Lend ENSA', presumably because we were lent

32

to ENSA by the Rep. For some reason this gave us a seemingly higher status, and we had a few extra privileges, such as being fitted with officers' uniforms made by Simpson's, and being allowed to use the Officers' Clubs. We heard that we were going abroad.

It was rumoured that we were going to Italy, but we left King's Cross station at midnight one night, not knowing where the train was taking us. Everything was very secretive in wartime, but eventually our destination was confirmed as Italy. We ended up in Greenock, which seemed a funny way of getting to Italy, and spent all the next day on board a very small ship, waking up in the middle of the night, seasick and on our way. I never saw the dining-room for the whole of the two-week trip, and had no desire to do so. I mostly lay on my bunk, sucking barley sugars and growing very slim. On my tottery little excursions on deck I got to know two very charming and beautiful girls called Kim and Kay Kendall, who were going out to join a concert party.

Many years later Kay was to become quite a fan of mine and the show I was in, *Living for Pleasure* at the Garrick Theatre in London. She was married to Rex Harrison, who was having a long run as Professor Higgins in *My Fair Lady* at the Theatre Royal, Drury Lane. Kay passed her evenings watching other shows. She came to *Living for Pleasure* many, many times. She would have a box, and bring all her famous friends to see us. David Niven was one. Then she would come round backstage, singing all the numbers. She badly wanted to be in the show, she said, and had even asked the management if she could. She would have been wonderful. She said she only wanted pin money, but nothing came of it. Perhaps Rex had said No. We found out later, however, that he knew then that she was dying of leukaemia. Poor beautiful Kay.

In spite of the rough transport and rather primitive hostels we had to put up with, I thoroughly enjoyed that ENSA tour. When we played under canvas in makeshift theatres and saw what the troops were having to endure, we knew we were the lucky ones, even though we sometimes had to sleep seven to a room. My first night in Naples was an introduction to what we would have to encounter in less palatial hostels later in the tour. I had to get up in the middle of the night to go to the bathroom, and, having reached it, groped around unsuccessfully for the light switch. I groped further, and somehow found the seat I required. Then as my eyes grew accustomed to the darkness I spotted the light switch above the wash basin, and flicked it on. I wished I hadn't because the floor of the bathroom was a seething mass of black beetles, and I realized I had crunched my way over them in my bare feet! I was so sickened and shocked that I jumped into the bath and screamed, and kept screaming until our leading man, Patrick Barton, heard the noise and came to rescue me.

What Naples lacked in cleanliness it made up for in other ways. There was the beautiful sunshine of course, but there were also some glamorous shops, where I promptly swapped my army issue brogues for a gorgeous pair of wedge-heeled sandals, which were all the rage at that time. We were supposed to wear our full uniform always, but we soon discovered that there was no one around who was really bothered about what the ENSA people were wearing. The weeks wore on, and we grew hotter and hotter in our regulation khaki, so our uniforms gradually became a strange mixture of bits and pieces — khaki skirts worn with silk blouses and wedge-heeled sandals were quite popular. I wasn't used to army style protocol, and on our first day in Naples, when we were shopping in the Via Roma, we were still at the stage of wearing full and correct uniform. There I was, resplendent in my Simpson's tailored officer's uniform, and a passing ATS girl saluted me. I was so surprised that without thinking I curtseyed. Goodness knows what she thought.

The heat was intense, and on at least one occasion caused me great embarrassment. We were playing J.B. Priestley's *Dangerous Corner* to some troops just outside Foggia, in southern Italy. I was wearing a long pink crêpe evening dress, cut on the cross, and slim-fitting. Although *Dangerous Corner* is a good play, there is very little action and a lot of talking. I had to sit through a long, typically wordy, Priestley scene, in which I occupied centre stage. By the time I stood up to make my exit I found that I was so hot and wet from sitting still that my long slimline pink crêpe evening dress had shrunk and transformed itself into a skin-tight, damply clinging *short* evening dress.

We sometimes played to American troops, and although they were extremely nice, they were apt to be a little high-spirited. We happened to be playing at an American camp on VE night, and they became so carried away with their celebrations that they set fire to the tents. One of their great attributes was generosity. As I didn't drink wine or spirits, and we weren't allowed to drink the water, I often went thirsty, as there wasn't any alternative. If we played to the Americans they were always good for a few bottles of Coca Cola. I swapped one bottle of my NAAFI whisky ration for a copy of *Forever Amber*, which was banned in England at that time, and both parties involved in the exchange thought they'd pulled off a marvellous deal. I couldn't wait to get my hands on the book, and the Yank was highly delighted with his extra bottle of Scotch, so Lease-Lend took on a whole new meaning.

It was a wonderful atmosphere in Italy, and the

longer we stayed, the better I began to like it. By the time we had to leave to return to Colchester and weekly rep, I didn't want to go back at all. I begged and pleaded with our producer, Robert Digby, to be allowed to stay behind and join the Combined Services. Everything in me which was remotely actressy rose to the surface as I told him dramatically that he couldn't possibly know how much I loved the sunshine after the fog and cold in which I'd been brought up in Lancashire. And anyway, I added patriotically, the troops *needed* us. It was a lovely performance I gave him, but, alas, it fell upon stony ground. We had to go back to England, so we sailed on the *Empress of Scotland* in the last convoy of the war, and arrived in Liverpool in pouring rain, to be greeted like conquering heroes by all the civic dignitaries and a brass band playing Noël Coward's 'Mad Dogs and Englishmen', but there wasn't much mid-day sun about at the time. I caught a train back to Oldham and showed off my sun-tan to everyone. It was much admired and envied of course, but Mum had certain reservations. She was terribly upset because my hair, which had been bleached almost white by the Italian sun, was quite a different colour from what it had been when I left. This could only mean one thing as far as Mum was concerned — I must have been 'tampering with it', and I had a hard job convincing her that the bleaching process was entirely due to the sun, and not to the contents of a bottle of peroxide.

I was so happy to see my parents and Bill again that I soon forgot all that big scene in Italy when I had pleaded to be left behind. Now that I was back among them all, it almost seemed like an act of treachery. There was no place like home, and, as far as I was concerned, there never would be. Bill couldn't believe that I hadn't fallen for some glamorous uniformed Adonis while I was away, but little did he realize that when you're playing at a different camp every night, there is only ever time to say Hello and Goodbye to people. Still, I was secretly pleased that he was showing some signs of jealousy. I was also very pleased to find that I'd managed to save £70 out of my ENSA salary, so after playing out my contract with Colchester Rep, I decided that with all this money I could afford to live in London and look for a job there. It seemed a marvellous idea, but I had reckoned without the Inland Revenue. Out of the blue came a summons to an interview at Colchester Income Tax Office, where I was asked very firmly why I had never paid any income tax.

It was a good question, but I had a perfectly good answer. 'Because nobody has ever asked me to,' I replied with genuine innocence. This was absolutely true, and I wasn't trying to be funny. If anyone had asked me for income tax, I'd have paid it, but I hadn't been asked. My reply did not appear to satisfy the questioner, who told me that it was my responsibility to offer the money anyway.

'But nobody in their right mind goes and says, "Can I pay my income tax?" ' I said to the tax official, who obviously did not agree with this point of view, and indicated that the country was full of honest people, all rushing to their local tax offices to pay their dues. Further questions as to my previous whereabouts revealed that I had been moving around so much that they had never caught up with me. 'Well, that wasn't my fault, was it?' I asked defensively. That didn't go down too well. 'So whose fault was it then?' he wanted to know.

It was an awful interview, which ended in tears as I was coldly informed that I had to pay £100 in back tax. He might just as well have said £1,000. That squashed my lovely idea of going to London. I had visions of being forced to stay in Colchester for the rest of my life, paying off the Inland Revenue.

I had never before asked my parents for a penny, as I knew what sacrifices my mother had to make to enable me to get so far, but Mum knew of my plans to go to London with my seventy pounds of ENSA money, so I had to tell Mum and Dad that I now wouldn't be able to go. Once more I had cause to thank God for parents like mine, because Mum said, 'Dora, you know the two pounds a week you've been sending home to us for the last two years, ever since you left? Well, your dad and I have been saving it for you in case you might need it. Now I think the time has come.'

So there was to be no going back. I had already given in my notice at Colchester Rep before the income tax man had sent for me. All I had to do now was to find somewhere to live in the Big City. I had not thought of going to my auntie in Ilford, knowing she couldn't possibly put up with me indefinitely as she had two grown-up sons, but I knew that at least she would always be good for a tuck-in on Sundays. In the meantime I would just have to start looking around.

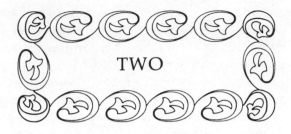

TWO

I KNEW ONLY ONE OTHER PERSON IN LONDON, AND THAT was my friend Harald Melvill, who had been scenic artist at Oldham Rep. I wrote to him and asked if he could help.

Harald replied saying how happy he was that I was coming to try my luck in London, and that the only room he knew of was in the same house as his. It was the attic, five floors up, and was only used as a store room. It had no running water, but it did at least have a bed and a wash-stand, and the landlord had said I could have it for 7s.6d. a week if I was willing to tidy it up. It wasn't exactly the Ritz, but it sounded lovely to me, so after a weekend at home I arrived in London.

Harald had already tried to sort out the room for me, but it was still full of junk, and in the middle of all the junk was a bed. If I leaned out of the window there was also a view of Hampstead Heath. I was very thrilled with my first London home. My landlord, Mr Jones, was on the top floor, and a sweet lady called Mrs Pettit — a vicar's widow — had the other room. If Mr Jones was in a good mood he would let us fill our water jugs from the tap in his room, instead of going down two

39

flights of badly lit stairs. Mrs Pettit and I became very good friends, and we would invite each other to little tea parties, asking Harald and our landlord to join us. I did wonders on my gas ring, and Mum came to visit and did a spot of decorating. In these days of Do-It-Yourself marvels we have the benefit of emulsion paints, but in those days it was a powdery concoction called distemper which was used on ceilings and walls. Mum distempered the walls pale blue, and Harald very kindly painted all the woodwork white for me. Unknown to Mr Jones, we also surreptitiously disposed of a lot of the junk down to the basement.

With £70 in the bank and a lovely home, who could wish for more? Well, perhaps a job would not come amiss, so I copied a list of agents from *Spotlight*, the theatrical advertising and casting book, and wrote dozens of letters asking for interviews. The replies duly came back, and they all said the same thing, to the effect: 'When you get a job, let me know, and I will come and see you work.' It was like the eternal conundrum about which came first — the chicken or the egg. How did I get a job if I hadn't an agent, and how did I get an agent unless I had a job? Time was passing, and the £70 bank balance was steadily being depleted. I was so thrilled to be in London that I was going to see shows, and treating myself to a delicious little supper at a Corner House afterwards. All this riotous living meant that I had to keep going to the post office to take out a bit more money. I had also added a few refinements to my flatlet, as I called it, and had bought new curtains, and a camp bed for when Mum came to stay. Then there were some cooking utensils needed, and a little tea service for entertaining Mrs Pettit and Harald, so the money was dwindling with alarming rapidity.

Harald's job at that time was as scenic artist at the New Lindsey Theatre in Notting Hill Gate, and one evening he came rushing up to my room to ask if I could remember the part of Nancy in the play *Gaslight*, which I had done some years previously at Oldham Rep. I said that I could remember it vaguely, and wondered why he wanted to know. He didn't waste much time. 'Here's a script,' he said, handing it over. 'Come with me to rehearsal tomorrow. The girl who should be doing the part is ill, and I've told them I know someone who can do it. We open tomorrow night.'

I was certainly taken aback by this sudden turn of events, but as I have always found it very easy to learn lines I had no nerves at all about that side of things. The only thing that kept me awake that night was a nagging worry that the other girl might make a miraculous recovery. But it's an ill wind . . . etc., and luck was definitely on my side. I arrived at rehearsal, and the part was mine. I had a job in London, even if it wasn't in the West End, and I was very grateful. During the day I found time to phone as many agents as possible of those I had written to, asking them to come and see my London début. Of course it was very short notice, but they all promised to come. Not one of them turned up, needless to say. However, the girl whose place I had taken did me yet another favour. Firth Shephard's casting director was looking for girls for the play *Stage Door*, and he had already arranged to come and see her that night. As she was ill, he saw me instead, and when he came backstage he thought at first I was the girl who had written to him. After we'd settled the problem of mistaken identity, he asked me to attend an audition the following day. As *Gaslight* was only a three-week season, and my salary was just £3 a week, I needed another job as soon as I could find one. This seemed providential. I was convinced that if I did a play for Firth Shephard it would run for ever, as he had a run of very successful plays.

41

I think I'm right in saying that I attended ten auditions during the course of which I read for every girl's part in *Stage Door*. As there were about twenty parts I almost made a full-time career of attending auditions. Years later I found out from Coral Browne, who was a good friend of Firth Shephard at the time, that he was determined to give me a part, but as I had read them all well, he was confused as to which one to give me. If only I had known that at the time I would have been able to sleep at nights. Because I could dance, the final decision was to give me the part of Pat, who at one point in the play had to do a cartwheel across the stage. So at last I had my part in the West End, and I thought that Dora Bryan had finally arrived.

It was all very well to be cartwheeling about the West End, but the trouble was that it was a whole month before we were due to start rehearsals, and in the meantime I had worked my way through the whole of my precious £70. After I had signed my contract with Firth Shephard I wrote to Oldham Rep to see if they could use me for a week or two, so that I might make up my depleted bank balance. They replied that they could. They were doing a try-out of a new play by Walter Greenwood, *So Brief the Spring*, with Robert Newton as guest star. Would I like to go back for £12 a week, and also do a further week in another play, *A Soldier for Christmas*? I was thrilled. Two weeks at home, with pay, and a chance to work with a wonderful actor like Robert Newton into the bargain. A charming man, but little did I know what was to be in store for me when I worked with him.

Bob had just come out of the navy, and it was no secret that he had an affection for alcohol. This had its problems for everyone, not least for me, as all my scenes in the play were with him. It was very nerve-racking, because he would arrive on stage having had a

42

sustaining amount of drink, and at times was so incoherent that he couldn't really be understood, and invariably I found myself having to say his lines as well as my own. He also took it upon himself to rearrange the plot of the play. I was playing the part of the hussy, and he took quite a fancy to me, making wild grabs at me on stage instead of lavishing his attentions upon the character supposed to be his true love. This made no sense of the production at all, and when dear Walter Greenwood came to see his play for the first time he wondered what on earth had happened to it.

One night after the show Bob offered to give me a lift home in his taxi. He was staying at the Midland Hotel in Manchester. We drew up at our gate just as Mum and Dad were going in with fish and chips, so Dad invited Mr Newton in for a cup of tea. The taxi was disposed of, and we went inside. Bob said he didn't like tea very much, and added that he was actually allergic to it, so instead he worked his way through Dad's bottle of Drambuie. Just after the war, that was a luxury ordinary people saved for Christmas, but for Bob it was Christmas every day, and the bottle disappeared in one evening. I left them to it and went off to bed, as I had to be up early for rehearsal the next day, and had to learn my lines for *A Soldier for Christmas*. I had switched off the light and was about to go to sleep when I saw a large figure in long naval underwear silhouetted against the doorway, and making its way towards me. Fortunately Dad had heard somebody moving about and came to the rescue, intent upon preserving the chastity of his only daughter. 'No, Mr Newton,' he said, kindly but very firmly. 'You're sleeping in here.' And he propelled Bob towards his allotted bedroom, which was my brother's room, John still being away in the navy.

I met Bob again years later, when I was in revue in

London. He was ill and stone-cold sober. He kept looking at me in a puzzled sort of way and said, 'I've a feeling I've met you before somewhere.' I didn't enlighten him, but I'm sure he didn't know that he'd ever been to such a place as Oldham Rep for a special week, or that he'd ever spent a night in our house. There were many stories about the adventures of Robert Newton, but my favourite story was told to me by a taxi driver who was detailed to look after him during the making of a film. Not only did the taxi driver have to convey him from place to place, but he also had to keep an eye on him, as Bob was going through one of his notorious 'bad patches'. He had finished filming at Pinewood Studios one evening, and the taxi driver was waiting for him, as arranged, to take him safely back to his hotel. But Bob emerged from the studios, got into the car, and barked out 'Portsmouth'. The driver was surprised, but knew better than to offer an argument, so he duly drove off in the direction of Portsmouth, where Bob said, 'Dockside', and alighted alongside one of the big ships there. After a bit of trouble with the man in charge, Bob then walked up the gangway of the ship and wasn't seen until 6.30 the following morning. The driver patiently waited for him all night, and when Bob hove into view he got into the car, sank into the back seat and said, 'Pinewood'. He had been for a night out with his old shipmates, which seemed to him to be the most natural thing in the world.

After my two weeks at Oldham I reported for rehearsals for *Stage Door*, which starred Patricia Burke and Bernard Lee. Bernard had just come out of the army, and I was to work with him again — all too soon, as it happened — in *Peace in Our Time* by Noël Coward. I say it was all too soon because my fond hopes of a long run in *Stage Door* were dashed. It only ran for six weeks. Fortunately I had been seen in it by Daphne

Rye, who was casting director for H.M. Tennent, and I was asked to audition for the part of Sybil in a tour of Coward's *Private Lives*. It had been successfully revived in the West End with Googie Withers in the Gertrude Lawrence role, and they wanted to send it on tour. I got the part, and did a long tour of places like Minehead, Ilfracombe, and Shanklin on the Isle of Wight, where no one came to see us as it was November, and they switched off all the lights on the island at eight o'clock. Still, it was very useful to work for Tennents, and I was now able to speak of 'Binkie' as a person. I don't think he actually ever saw me in the play, but at least he was paying my salary, which gave the relationship a personal touch.

After the tour it was back to London again, and a search for work. By this time my friend Sarah had decided to try her luck in London, and had found a flat just off Harley Street, but as the rent was four guineas a week she needed someone to share it with her. She asked me, and so I left my happy home in Hampstead, not without a few regrets, and moved in with her.

Soon after I moved in, my brother John came to stay the night with us. He was on his way to Southampton to meet his fiancée. As a captain in the Fleet Air Arm he had met this young lady in Cape Town, and three days later, just before he sailed for home, they had become engaged. Now she was coming to England, and it was an anxious-looking brother who set off for Southampton that morning, to meet her from the boat. But later in the day came a phone call to say, 'Everything's fine. She's even more beautiful than I remembered.' Within two months they were married, and within a year Marguerite, my beautiful sister-in-law, was expecting the first of three lovely daughters, and they decided to go back to South Africa to live. I was sad to see them go, but I had my career and my own life to lead. My parents were sad to say goodbye again to their only son, after four years of naval service, to say nothing of their new daughter-in-law and a grandchild on the way.

It did not take very long for Sarah and me to discover that two guineas a week each was quite a lot of money to find for rent, so we decided to be enterprising and take in a lodger at three guineas a week, bed and breakfast. It meant a little bit of inconvenience for us, but we thought it worthwhile. Sarah and I moved in and shared the second bedroom, and took it in turns to get up and cook the lodger's breakfast. We had several lodgers, and the snag was that our wide variety of paying guests all had their own ideas of what added up to three guineas' worth. Among them was an actress, who had to be given her marching orders because she had too many boy friends. We found that we were always having to cook two breakfasts instead of one, and economically that just didn't work out. Then Sarah's boy friend moved in, and as he apparently didn't qualify to pay any rent at all, I moved out.

During all this time in flats I managed to spend the odd brief weekend at home with Mum and Dad, and make a fleeting visit to Bill. I did look forward to those weekends. Dad would be waiting to meet me from the Euston to Manchester train, and the weekend would pass in a haze of food, comfort, warmth, and love. Then it was back to London in time for the Monday evening show, with a few tears, and a pound of sugar, some butter, and perhaps some chocolate as a treat. These things were hard to come by, as rationing was still in progress, and my solitary ration card did not have much purchasing power. On other Sundays, when I couldn't afford the fare to Oldham, I'd be on the 25B bus to Ilford, to Auntie May's, to fill up with food and bring a bit back.

After I had taken my departure from the flat I shared with Sarah and the lodgers I found myself a bed-sitter in an elderly gentleman's flat in Southampton Row for twenty-five shillings a week, with the use of the kitchen and bathroom. I persuaded another girl friend to take a room there too, to keep me company, and we set up house with Mr Mason, our landlord. This worked out very well. My friend and I, together with Mr Mason, pooled our rations, because it made everything go further, but when they discovered my large appetite we decided it was fairer to keep the rations of butter, sugar and tea in our own rooms. Mr Mason was quite a nice man, but a bit mean about electricity. I swear he sat up all night watching the electricity meter in case I put the fire on.

We had a lovely big kitchen in the flat, and as I've always been fond of cooking I really went to town, creating amazing cakes with saccharin and dried eggs, because the sugar ration would not run to cakes, and eggs were hard to come by. I did have one major failure however, and I have to confess that the marmalade I made with saccharin was not too successful. My first cake nearly resulted in my friend Grace losing a tooth. It wasn't that the cake was hard, but our utensils left something to be desired. The trouble was that Mr Mason never cooked for himself, and although he had all the necessary equipment tucked away, he used the various receptacles for his own household purposes. He had made the discovery that his cake tins were perfect for keeping items like tin tacks, and consequently one of my cakes contained a flavoursome tin tack, as Grace discovered when she took a bite. She generously forgave me, and gave me a beautiful cookery book for my birthday, but she couldn't resist writing in it: 'For my friend Dora, and in which there is no mention of tin tacks.'

In between bouts of cooking I was busy looking for work, and after an audition I took over from the late Joan Dowling in *No Room at the Inn*. This was a very good play about wartime evacuees, and I played the part of Norma, the precocious thirteen-year-old cockney kid. It was a marvellous part, and that fine actress Freda Jackson played the harridan of a foster mother, who took the London evacuees into her home. Her performance was so convincing, and worked the audience into such a frenzy of hatred for her that one night in the famous scene where she got very drunk, and vented her temper on the terrified children in her charge, she spoke her line, 'I don't half feel bad,' and a voice from the gallery shouted, 'And so you bloody well should!' Freda Jackson and Joan Dowling later re-created their roles in the film with great success, and they wrote a nice part in the film for me — a tart, as usual! Although by now I was twenty-two years old, when I was wearing children's clothes, and my face was devoid of any make-up I somehow managed to look not a day older than thirteen, the age of Norma, the character I was playing. My real age came as quite a shock to Jack Hylton, who was presenting the play. I had been engaged for the part by Anthony Hawtrey, and Jack Hylton had only seen me on stage. When he gave a party to celebrate a year's run of the play, he didn't recognize me in my sophisticated black chiffon dress and high heels, and even asked me if I was an actress.

After the West End run of *No Room at the Inn* we took it on tour, and while playing in Brighton I had a call from Daphne Rye of H.M. Tennent, to ask if I could go to London to attend an audition for a new Noël Coward play, *Peace in Our Time*, which was about what would have happened if Germany had won the war and occupied England. I was given the lovely little part of Phyllis, the barmaid, and really felt that I was getting somewhere. I could now add 'Noël' as well as 'Binkie' to my repertoire of names worth dropping. Again I found myself working with Bernard Lee, and another member of the cast was Kenneth More. Noël would terrify us all by giving us notes after the performance. The first time this happened we were all called on to the stage after the show, and we stood about waiting for him. He went round all the members of the cast one by one, and tore strips off everyone with his acid tongue. When would he get to me, and what would he say? I was trembling, and my ears were singing with terror. I was the last. Eventually he turned to me and said in those familiar clipped tones, 'And as for you, Dora Bryan — whoever taught you to make up with those George Robey eyebrows didn't bargain for the fact that you can't keep them still. It's very distracting for the audience, especially as you never stop acting with them while other people are speaking.' I vaguely wondered why nobody had complained before, but I certainly learned my lesson. I never made up my eyebrows in the show after that little homily, and as they are as blonde as my hair, I must have looked very bald. Still, at least it was only my make-up he had criticized, I consoled myself.

That was a very lucky play for me, because while I was in it I was seen by two important people. One was an agent called Herbert de Leon, who said he would like to put me under contract, and the other one was the film director Carol Reed. He gave me a small part in his film *Odd Man Out*, and this was followed by another small part in *The Fallen Idol*, in which I played the role of a street walker who befriended the little French boy, played by Bobby Henrey. The two stars of the film were Ralph Richardson and Michelle Morgan. I was very fortunate to have had a director like Carol Reed. I'd never heard of 'method acting' or improvisation, and

49

this was the nearest thing to it. The technique of filming was entirely different from theatre work. For one thing I found that I didn't have to think of the people sitting up in the 'gods', and have to project my voice and keep my chin up. The cameras were so close that they could pick out the flicker of an eyelash, and the microphones so sensitive that they would react to the tiniest whisper. I had no script, and was told by Carol Reed to put the whole scene into my own words. It was a scene at a police station, and the police had called upon Rosie, the prostitute, to come in and help to question the small French boy who had been found wandering the streets in his pyjamas. Rosie makes friends with the little boy, and when she finds out that he lives at the French Embassy, and that his father is the French Ambassador, she says, 'Oh, I know your daddy.' With Carol Reed's help, the whole improvisation of the scene seemed to work.

As I was playing the role of a tart, I was not particularly flattered when he said that the clothes I was already wearing would be just right. They were my own, and I was wearing my best little red suit! He compromised by letting me wear a plastic mac over it, but even so, I didn't feel exactly happy. A similar experience came some time later when I was rehearsing an Emlyn Williams play, *Accolade*, at the Aldwych Theatre. Again I was playing a prostitute, this time an amateur one — she just liked it, and her husband didn't mind. Lily Taylor, the wardrobe mistress for H.M. Tennent, went shopping with me for my clothes for the play. We went along Oxford Street and bought some real beauties — lurex and satins in hideous colours, and at the dress parade before the dress rehearsal I proudly showed off all these terrible clothes that Lily and I had so carefully chosen. 'No, no!' shouted our director, Glen Byam Shaw, when he saw them. 'They won't do at all. I want Dora to look just as she does at rehearsals.' Shattering. I'd always thought I had such a good taste in clothes.

Although I did only two days' work on *The Fallen Idol* I certainly learned a lot about filming, even if I never learned my way around Shepperton Studios. I arrived very late on my first morning. My call had been for 7 a.m. in the make-up department, so I had set my alarm for 5 a.m., and travelled by train to Shepperton, where I set off down the main street to find the studios, quite sure that they would be just around the corner. As it turned out, they proved to be a mile and a half away, and I had to walk. I found myself ploughing across snowy fields on both days, and I was late on both days. I later learned that there was a special bus which took the film people from the London train to the studios. How I wished somebody had told me before, but nobody seemed to mind too much that I was late. Quite different from nowadays, when there is some-times only a six-week schedule. At the time of *The Fallen Idol* a perfectly ordinary film could take three months or more. We were held up for two weeks because little Bobby Henrey's mother unthinkingly took him to have his hair cut one weekend, and he arrived at the studios on the Monday morning with his hair an inch shorter. As the scene they were shooting ran in strict continuity with the last shot they had filmed on the Friday, they had to wait two weeks for Bobby's hair to grow again.

My first great break in films came with Walter Greenwood's Lancashire comedy *The Cure for Love*, starring Robert Donat, who also directed it. My studio call was for 7 a.m. each day, but I never did a thing until after lunch. Robert Donat suffered terribly from asthma, and he was often far from well while we were making that film. Some days he couldn't work at all, but we all had to be ready in case it was one of his good days. My routine was to get made up, have my hair done, and then go back to bed on my dressing room divan until I was called. As I was also playing in *Traveller's Joy* each night at the Criterion Theatre, and playing a small part in the film of *The Blue Lamp*, I really was becoming rather tired, and the lure of that dressing room divan was quite irresistible, with its promise of a little much needed sleep. Renée Asherson, Robert Donat's real-life girl friend, and later his wife, played Milly, the nice pleasant heroine of the piece, and I was cast as Janey Jenkins, Robert's deliciously common 'feeancy', who had somehow been wished upon him before he met Milly. Robert played the part of Jack Hardacre, a Lancashire soldier home on leave. In Janey's words she had been 'three years and faithful'. She was loud, tarty, and quite awful, so her gem of a line to her mother (Gladys Henson), 'Don't be so common, Mother!' always seemed doubly funny. Jack's mother was played by Marjorie Rhodes, and Jack's dilemma arose when he came home on leave and fell in love with Milly, who had been billeted on his mother during his absence. How could he get rid of Janey? My 'three years and faithful' line didn't hold any water, as there were too many shots of me running in and out of air raid shelters with Polish airmen. Gladys and I were terrible gigglers, and so was Robert when he had scenes with the two of us. He could never look at this gruesome twosome without a snigger, so he would look straight past us, which only made things worse. He ruined so many scenes by laughing until he cried, that when we reached Take 26 we would have to cancel shooting for the day and retire to our dressing rooms in disgrace.

Robert decided that my physique was not quite what he had in mind for the ghastly Janey Jenkins, and he wanted her to have a little more upholstery above the belt than Dora Bryan had been endowed with. The result was that one glorious day he took me to have some falsies 'constructed' (and there was no other word for it), by a sculptor of some kind. I don't quite know what he was, but he made me the most ridiculous bra arrangement out of rubber. The indignity of the whole thing was that I had to stand around in my own bra while Robert and this sculptor fellow discussed and shaped my new chest quite clinically, building it up with a plaster which they moulded on to me. My own bra was a write-off after this, as it was covered with all this muddy stuff. Robert thought he would like a lemon shape, and the other man said he thought an orange shape with a nipple would be better. So at one moment of sheer madness I was standing there — oranges and lemons personified — with one orange-shaped boob with a nipple on the end of it, while the other one was a lemon. I didn't have quite so much sense of humour in those days, and I felt both embarrassed and ridiculous. The mould was taken away when it had been completed, and was used as a base for the bra which I was supposed to wear in the film. Nobody found out that I never did wear it, but wore my own bra, and padded it with as much cotton wool as I could find, rather than wear that awful thing with the false nipples. I can see it now, hanging up, with all the little holes in it so that I could 'breathe'.

The Cure for Love, I may say, was the film that was going to make me into the Big Star. I was heading for a contract with MGM. Oh yes, I thought, when I made that film all the Hollywood studios would be fighting over me. Despite all the English films I'd made, nobody here had discovered me as yet. But this big star Robert Donat had discovered me, so Hollywood was going to be next. I had it all worked out. When the film was finished it was given a special press preview before going on general release. Everyone was optimistic. Gladys and I went to the morning press show, feeling sure we would come out glowing with success. But the film was received in total silence, so we crept away and left Robert to talk to the press at the reception. Gladys took me to Rules Restaurant in Maiden Lane, and introduced me to martini cocktails. The notices for the film were unbelievably bad. I didn't even want to go out, let alone be discovered! Gladys and I were referred to as 'Bud Abbott and Lou Costello with clogs on', among other things. I just felt the whole world would know about our gigantic flop, and I was glad to creep through the stage door of the Criterion Theatre and the security and success of *Traveller's Joy*. Amazingly, although London hated the film, and the run at the Odeon, Leicester Square, had to be curtailed, from Birmingham northwards we were a huge success, and had long runs in the cinemas in the north. In Newcastle it ran for eighteen weeks.

All this racing about between film studios and theatres really did begin to take its toll of my energy. Most of the scenes for *The Blue Lamp* were filmed late at night, which meant working for days and nights without sleep. I found myself dropping off in the car which took me to and fro. No wonder Yvonne Arnaud, with whom I was appearing in *Traveller's Joy*, telephoned the management to report, 'Poor leetle Dora is so tired. She is yawning on ze stage.' The management didn't take too kindly to that sort of thing, so they stepped in and barred me from doing any more filming while I was in the play. I wasn't very pleased about that, but from a health point of view it was probably a good thing that I stopped when I did.

After the opening of *Traveller's Joy* my friend Nancy and I were invited to a new club, the White Room. It was in Denman Street in Soho, the street where the Piccadilly Theatre is. The White Room was up a few steps at Number 19, and was a very pleasant theatrical club with an excellent pianist and a charming manager, Ralph Saunders. Nancy and I were enrolled as members, and during the course of conversation I happened to say I was looking for a flat. 'Come upstairs,' said Ralph. It seemed a funny thing to say, so I grabbed Nancy for protection, and we went up two flights of stairs. There, for four guineas a week, was a self-contained, nicely furnished flat. It seemed that the previous tenants had been ladies of easy virtue who paid three times that amount, but the new landlord had moved them out. I was so thrilled with my new home. After sharing with Mr Mason and Grace it was wonderful to have my own West End flat. My cousin Keith and I painted all the woodwork eau-de-Nil, and each night I arrived at the theatre covered with splashes of pale green paint. I was to stay in that flat for three years, and would have been there longer but for an incident with my father.

My parents came to stay with me for a few days, which meant that I had to sleep in the sitting room. It was summer, and one very hot night the windows were wide open. The music from Buddy Bradley's club just across the road was floating in. Down in the street a news vendor was shouting, 'Late night final!' so Dad said he would just pop down and buy the evening paper to see how Oldham Athletic had got on that day. After some time he came back, looking rather strange, and without a paper.

'Where's the paper?' I asked.

'Oh, they've sold out,' he replied briefly.

I thought that was odd, because I could still hear the man shouting, 'Late night final!' but Dad would not be drawn any further so the matter was dropped. I

found out weeks later the reason for his strange behaviour. The papers were Polish papers, and weren't
for sale as papers, but they contained little packets of
what are discreetly referred to as rubber goods. Late
night final might indeed have been quite apt. Poor
Dad. He must have had an awful shock. After Oldham
Garden Suburb, Denman Street did seem a little daring,
with all the street girls and their boy friends. I was
never bothered by them. They would all say Hello to
me, and make a fuss of my little dog, a Sealyham called
Binkie, whom I'd named after Mr Beaumont, the managing director of H.M. Tennent. Sadly Binkie the dog
had to be put to sleep after three years because he
began to bite everyone — me mostly. I really loved it in
Denman Street, just a few hundred yards from the
theatres and the excitement of the West End. The White
Room flourished. Roger Moore was a frequent visitor.
Diana Dors would come in with her first husband,
Dennis Hamilton, and Joan Collins with her first husband, Maxwell Reed. If I wasn't filming during the day
my social life revolved around Nancy, my understudy
and best friend (who later was my bridesmaid), and
Derek and Ernst, our gay, and therefore strictly platonic
boy friends.

We would go to trade showings of the latest films in
the mornings, then in the afternoons I'd walk Binkie in
Green Park, and have tea at the S.F. Grill, opposite my
flat. The customers were mainly actors and actresses, in
or out of work, and the place was a mine of information
about auditions, what was going on where, and general
gossip. Where does everyone go to gossip now, I
wonder? On Fridays we would meet at the theatre to
collect our salary, and go off for coffee at Fortnum and
Mason because we felt rich. If I wanted to eat out at that
time I mostly went to the Vega Restaurant in Leicester
Square. It was a vegetarian restaurant, and they very

kindly allowed me to take my dog Binkie in with me. He had his own plate, and we would have a jolly good healthy lunch for five shillings. Translated into new currency this hardly seems possible. Where could you go today and have a full-scale lunch for 25 pence? Meat rationing was still in operation when I was living in Denman Street, and eating at the vegetarian restaurant meant that I could save my precious meat coupon (worth two ounces), for the weekend. Two ounces of meat was usually two slices of corned beef, or a small chop if the butcher was feeling generous. The interesting thing is that we were all much healthier in those days of rationing, and the spartan diet must have suited us.

Alas, my days in Denman Street were to draw to a close. Mum had a word with me and said that Dad didn't think it was a suitable area for a girl to be living alone. After much heart-searching I capitulated, and moved to Queen Anne Mews, off Harley Street. That was all very pleasant, of course, but I did enjoy my time in Soho. I used to grow herbs in my window box, and if ever I walk along Denman Street these days I look up at the flat with a certain nostalgia. That window box is still there.

While playing in *Traveller's Joy* I shared a dressing room with Billie Hill, who was Yvonne Arnaud's understudy. Billie was a devout Christian Scientist, and dismissed colds in the head as 'pepper up her nose'. She was convinced that any illness she suffered must be some kind of error on her part. She lived a long and healthy life, and was a good advertisement for the theories and philosophy of Mary Baker Eddy.

Arthur Macrae, who had written *Traveller's Joy*, was also playing a part in it. He and I got along very well, and he eventually wrote a lot of songs and sketches for *The Lyric Revue*, *The Globe Revue* and *Living for Pleasure*.

57

One sketch in particular was brilliant, and he told me it was inspired by Vivien Leigh's bedroom. She had shown him her bedroom in her new flat in Eaton Place. The walls were decorated with a wallpaper full of roses, and the carpet, curtains and bedspread were all exactly the same. Arthur said all it needed was for the Spectre de la Rose to fly in through the window. So with the Weber music 'Invitation to the Dance' playing, which was used for the ballet *Le Spectre de la Rose*, I mimed the role of a young girl being shown into a hotel bedroom (decorated just like Vivien's), and at the appropriate moment in the music, in through the window leapt dancer Terry Skelton, dressed as the Spectre. In a great burlesque of the original ballet, he proceeds to whirl her into the dance, and eventually wins her over completely. She then chases him frantically around the stage until he manages to make a getaway by leaping out of the window. He is closely followed by the infatuated girl, whose leap is anything but silent, and is accompanied by the sound of shattering glass. It was a very funny sketch, and was repeated in a pantomime I did at a much later date at the London Hippodrome and at the Hippodrome in Bristol.

Arthur also wrote such sketches as 'Information Desk', in which the stupid receptionist at a smart London hotel gives the most extraordinary information to the guests over the internal telephone. She gives directions for Buckingham Palace as 'a stone's throw from Gorringe's', Kensington Palace can be found 'sort of behind Pontings', and it's no problem to find Westminster Abbey because it's 'near the Army and Navy Stores'. Giving French tourists information about current West End plays, *Seagulls Over Sorrento* became 'Les oiseaux au dessus de Sorrento' put on by 'Emile Plus Petit' (Emile Littler). She then has to ask her friend, 'Mavis, what's French for matinée?'

1. Aged 12. A Drury Lane Babe.

2. At the Oldham Rep in 1940.

Traveller's Joy ran for three years, including the tour. I played the part of the Swedish maid, Eva, and it was typical of all maids' parts. I could never leave the side of the stage because I had so many entrances and exits, so I occupied my time by knitting socks for all the male members of the cast. When they were satisfactorily stocked up, I started on the stage hands. It's surprising how much knitting one can get through in three years. In spite of Yvonne Arnaud temporarily curtailing my career in films because she thought I was about to fall asleep on the stage, I loved her. She was a great character and a marvellously funny actress. One of the things we had in common was a great love of animals. Her only vice — if it could be called that — was an absolute passion for food, and perhaps that chic but well-rounded figure was a testament to this obsession. On matinée days her dresser, Jessie, would arrive at the theatre with cake boxes packed with chocolate éclairs, meringues, and cream slices; all guaranteed to put on pounds in weight. The very first time I went into her dressing room between a matinée and an evening show, the table was so laden with scones, jam, honey and cakes that I thought she must be having guests, and I apologized for intruding on her party.

'But I am not expecting anyone, Dora dear,' she said with a bright smile. 'Do have an éclair.'

She really was delightful. I once bought a Persian lamb coat from her for £7, and for some strange reason it gradually turned the most peculiar shade of yellow. I have absolutely no idea why this should have happened, but I soon became the owner of the only yellow Persian lamb coat in London.

After three years I was released from my contract for *Traveller's Joy* to go into *Accolade* with Emlyn Williams and Diana Churchill. I played the prostitute, and this prompted a letter from my brother in South Africa who wrote, 'Can't you find yourself a part in which you're not a tart or a barmaid? I'm ashamed to admit that you're my sister! Why do you do it?'

I suppose I could have replied that I did it for the same reason as they did.

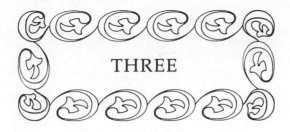

THREE

EMLYN WILLIAMS USED TO GIVE MARVELLOUS PARTIES during the run of *Accolade*. We took the play on tour before it opened in the West End, and he would often come back to the provincial digs I'd be sharing with one of the lesser paid members of the company, and I would make him laugh by doing some of the numbers I'd done as a child in pantomime or concert parties. I once gave Emlyn what he described as the best meal he'd had since the war. It consisted of cheese and onion pie and a flat currant cake.

Emlyn loved the introductory explanations I gave at these impromptu performances, describing what was happening on stage . . . 'Now — I'm dressed in Hungarian costume, dancing round a camp fire with a few other girls, and singing to the music of a Brahms Hungarian Dance:

> *"We are gay Hungarian girls*
> *Here at the fair.*
> *In our pretty national dress,*
> *Our high spirits*
> *No one can repress — OY!*

Come with us and join
The happy throng;
Come with us and sing
A merry song . . ." '

So it went on with more perfectly awful words. Then came a hectic dance routine with some tambourines. All those years after the original interpretation it seemed unbelievably corny. But Emlyn absolutely loved it, and thought it was one of the funniest things he'd ever seen. I also gave him my latter-day version of the routine with the xylophones strapped to my back, on which we had played the *Poet and Peasant* overture, which he found hilarious. When *Accolade* moved into the West End I was invited to one of Emlyn's famous parties. It seemed that every well-known star was there that night, including Bette Davis, Gary Merrill, Tyrone Power, Linda Christian, and many others. Also present was the great Binkie Beaumont of H.M. Tennent. Emlyn persuaded me to repeat some of my party pieces which he had seen me perform in my digs when we were on tour. His guests were a most appreciative audience, and on the strength of these solos, Binkie decided to put on a revue with a cast of comparative newcomers. So I found myself working with Ian Carmichael, Joan Heal, and Jeremy Hawk in what became *The Lyric Revue*.

Revue is slick and sophisticated, and it is not every theatre-goer's cup of tea. Certainly it didn't go down at all well in Cardiff, where we opened. We were a dreadful flop, and the management very nearly decided not to take it into London, but thank goodness they took the risk. The London audiences appreciated it, and we were a tremendous hit. On the opening night we took fourteen curtain calls, and we ran in the West End for two years.

The Lyric Revue was the first of three successful revues with the same principals in the cast, but two years later came the one in which I shared star billing with my great idol Hermione Baddeley and Ian Carmichael. That was called *At the Lyric*, which re-opened in 1954 at the St Martin's Theatre in a revised version called *Going to Town*. I loved being back in the musical theatre again — the overture, the opening chorus, the warmth of the audience, and especially the sense of freedom, which was indefinable, but it was all much more carefree than a straight play. I suppose in those days I did not have the sense of responsibility towards an audience that I have now. We learn a lot as the years advance, and it really is not done for the cast to have private little jokes on stage in which the audience has no part. I knew all that, of course, but those revues were all very funny, and members of the casts were all natural humorists, so a few giggles were inevitable. In a company which was constantly being admonished for giggling on stage I was the worst offender. I had only to catch the eye of Ian Carmichael or Graham Payn for disaster to threaten. Every week there would be statements that the curtain would be rung down on me if I could not curb my private sense of humour. Quite right, of course. It was very unprofessional.

My favourite sketch at that time, which the audiences loved, was the one in which I played the part of a child film star bemoaning her fate. At the age of eight she was already too old for the silver screen, and had to wear dark glasses to hide her premature wrinkles.

Richard Wattis was a delightful man, but he was very nervous when rehearsing his first revue with me. The rehearsals were hard work, and hectic, with new sketches to learn every five minutes, or so it seemed. I kept cheering up Dickie Wattis by saying, 'Never mind. Wait till we get to the band call. It will all come to life

63

and be marvellous. All the musical numbers we've been doing with just the piano will sound wonderful with the orchestra.' But band call came, and all my optimism was unfounded. Our opening number was a cacophony of wrong notes, and things went from bad to worse. Every number sounded as bad as the previous one. Poor Dickie was really depressed, but things improved before opening night. We had a duet which had been written by Alan Melville, called 'Cosette'. I wore a red wig, and a gorgeous red dress with hooks and eyes fastening it all down the back. Dickie wore an officer's dress uniform with gold braid and frogging across the chest. Our number was sung while I rested my back against his chest, swaying romantically. I was livid one evening because Dickie followed me offstage when I was supposed to exit alone. I thought he'd ruined everything, and decided that this time he'd really gone too far, until I discovered that he had had no option but to follow me, as we had become firmly hooked together, the hooks on the back of my dress having become badly entangled with the gold braid on his chest, so obviously, everywhere I went, he had to follow.

This sort of thing was not helpful towards keeping a straight face, and we had at least one disastrous performance in which we could not control ourselves at all. Again came the threat of the curtain being rung down, and there was quite a row. After the interval Dickie reappeared looking unnaturally solemn, the smile completely wiped from his face. 'I've taken three Libriums,' he announced in despair. 'I can do no more!'

During all the time I was having such success in London I was still seeing Bill regularly. He came to London for an occasional weekend, and we wrote to each other frequently, but marriage was still somewhere in the uncertain future. So we drifted along, sometimes breaking everything off for a time because it all seemed hopeless, and then inevitably coming back together again. There were problems on both sides. I could not pack up everything and go back to Oldham when things were going so well for me, and Bill couldn't give up his job at the big engineering firm of Ferranti, back in Oldham. He had also been playing professional football for Oldham Athletic, and professional cricket for St Anne's-on-Sea, but he decided to give up football and concentrate on cricket.

On one of his visits to London, nearly thirteen years after we had first met, we went out to Wimbledon Golf Club, where I had taken up golf. I may say here and now that my golfing was a complete waste of time. I spent a lot of money on fruitless lessons, and on golf balls, most of which are still in the lake. Bill was a good golfer, and he came round the Wimbledon course with me that morning, with my bags of clubs, and my poodle Sambo on a lead. He tried not to laugh at my pathetic efforts, and occasionally took a swipe at the ball with my driver, and was generally very patient. The one brilliant aspect of that morning's golfing was that we happened to run into Alf Gover, the England cricketer, whom Bill had played against many times in League cricket in the north. Alf had a very successful cricket school at Wandsworth, and while we were all having lunch at the clubhouse Alf said he was short of coaches at his school. Was Bill interested in a job there, he wanted to know.

It was, of course, just what we had always wanted; a job for Bill in London so that we could be together. He came to London and started working for Alf, and proved to be very good at the job. The prospects weren't exactly dazzling, but then, who wants to spend ten years waiting to become a foreman at Ferranti's, which is probably what would have happened if he had stayed in Oldham. As it was, everything was beginning to click into place. The next thing was to break the news to Mum and Dad that we wanted to get married. They came to London for Christmas that year, and must have sensed something, because after Christmas dinner, when we were all sitting around the fire in my little mews flat near Harley Street, Dad said suddenly, 'Don't you think it's about time you two got married?'

'As a matter of fact,' said Bill, 'I was just going to ask you about that.'

'Well, it's all right with me,' replied Dad, which meant that he had officially given his blessing. 'You'd better ask her mother.'

Bill didn't need to ask Mum, because by that time she had whipped out pencil and paper, and was already scribbling out a list of guests for the wedding. Mother was in charge, and from that moment everything was completely taken out of our hands. All we had to do was to make sure we got to Oldham, to St Thomas's Church, on 7 February 1954 — the wedding day, my birthday, and also a Sunday, as we were both working every other day. It was a marvellous wedding, and certainly a white one — snow white, as the snow was eight inches deep. Most of the cars couldn't get to the church, but I was lucky, as they put chains on the wheels, and we arrived without mishap. There were crowds outside, and I was surprised to see the police very much in evidence. But if I was conceited enough to believe that everyone had turned out to see me, I was soon brought down to earth and proved wrong by the headlines in some of the northern papers. Bill was also well known in the north. 'LAWTON WEDS ACTRESS' blazed out the headlines in large letters. That put things in perspective, I thought, and also put me firmly in my place.

Actually, Lawton very nearly didn't wed the actress that day, as the actress was at one time in grave danger of not being there. I had to catch the midnight train from Euston after Saturday night's show, and I was in my sleeper, undressed, with my wedding dress hanging up and my hair in pins. I'd smuggled Sambo, my poodle, in with me, and he was hiding under a blanket when the guard came round for the tickets. He looked at my ticket, scrutinising it carefully, and then said, 'You'll have to pay excess fare on this, Miss.'

'But that's ridiculous. I've only just bought it,' I protested.

'I can't help that, Miss. You can't go to Liverpool on a Manchester ticket.'

'I don't want to go to Liverpool!' I cried in horror. 'I want to go to Manchester!'

'Well, you'd better get off — quick,' said the man. 'This train's going to Liverpool. The Manchester sleeping cars are at the other end of the train. You've just about two minutes to get there.'

I have never moved so quickly in all my life. I swept up all my belongings, grabbed Sambo, and out I flew in my nightie, right down the platform with my wedding dress over my arm and Sambo barking at my heels. What would happen if I missed the train? ... No wedding ... everyone frantic ... complete disaster ... I must have presented an extraordinary picture running down that platform in my nightclothes, but I reached the right sleeper with less than a minute to spare. Sambo had caused such a commotion that there was no hope of sneaking him into the sleeper with me. I might have got away with it before, if we hadn't had to change sleeping cars, but this time there was no possibility of doing so.

'He goes in the luggage van,' said the guard firmly.

I said he wouldn't be any trouble, and that he was

used to being with me all the time, and that he wasn't a very big dog, and I made a heart-rending case for allowing him to sleep with me, but the guard refused to listen to all my pleas. The result was that I made myself a bed in the luggage van too, and lay down next to Sambo. What a wedding eve, I thought. The cruel guard ignored all this drama on my part for as long as he could, and kept walking past this dotty woman and her dog, bedded down in the luggage van. Then at last he relented and said, 'All right, miss. You win. Take him in the sleeper with you, but just remember that I haven't seen you.' So we transferred ourselves from the cold bleakness of the luggage van to the warmth of the sleeper. Not that I slept very much. The whole business had unnerved me. All this chopping and changing did nothing to contribute to the picture of tomorrow's tranquil and radiant bride, which I did so want to be. Things didn't improve very much when I reached Manchester early the next morning. Dad had to keep me waiting, as the snow was so deep that he couldn't possibly drive the car until a snow plough had cleared the way. It was a disastrous start to what turned out to be a wonderful day. All our good friends in the north were there, plus a lot of my London friends who had travelled up to be at my wedding. I suppose they thought much the same way as Dad did, after witnessing our ten-year courtship — 'About time too!'

It was the happiest day of my life, and I find it difficult to understand how any bride can bring herself to be married in a register office. The marriage service is so lovely. How could you possibly break those vows made in church? Bill looked as handsome as I had ever seen him, and when I reached the altar steps after almost running up the aisle on Dad's arm, he slyly whispered to me, 'Will I do?' Dear Bill — he certainly would do, and always has.

The reception was held at the largest hotel in Oldham, and this was followed by another party in the premises over the dress shop Mum had opened in Union Street. Having had a disturbed night, plus all the excitement and strain of the day, I was wilting a little by midnight, so we decided to leave for our honeymoon hotel. It was to have been the romantic Bells of Peover at Knutsford, but even our plans for that had to be changed at the last minute. Knutsford was snowed up and inaccessible, so we had to settle for the Midland Hotel in Manchester, where we were shown into what looked like a ballroom containing two single beds. We had borrowed Dad's car, and while Bill was putting it away for the night, I managed to organize another room for us, and moved in. It took Bill half the night to find me, because when he came back from putting the car away nobody at the reception desk thought to tell him that we'd moved, and he automatically went up to our original room. As I had disappeared he began to wander around looking for me, and searched almost the entire hotel. Then he was told the number of our new room, but by the time he found it I wasn't in there either. He had been away so long that I was starting to worry about him, and had gone off to try to find him. Our wedding night was beginning to take on all the aspects of a French farce, but we eventually found ourselves together in the same room some time after two o'clock in the morning, by which time I was ravenously hungry, as we hadn't eaten a thing since lunch. So we sat up in bed, ate chicken sandwiches and had a nice cup of tea, and decided it had been a lovely day.

The next day we returned to London. It was back to work for both of us, settling down as husband and wife, and when you've been used to pleasing yourself about everything this takes a lot of adjustment. When I was single, if I wanted to have lunch at four in the afternoon I could do so. Now I had a hungry man to look after, who happened to like his lunch at one o'clock. When he had done a hard day's coaching he couldn't stay up and go to parties with me, so I just didn't go any more. But the advantages outweighed everything else. I was no longer lonely. There were two of us now. Bill fitted in with my life, and I like to think I fitted in with his. I found I had a lot in common with other cricketers' wives, some of whom became my best friends. I schooled myself to become a good housewife, and I was also a very proficient plain cook.

Bill's cricketing career for a lot of the time was a mystery to me, as I was working in London and he played mainly in the north of England. When I had seen him play I was very impressed, particularly when in 1947 he played for Lancashire at Old Trafford against the Australians. If I wasn't working, and it was a nice day, I would take my knitting and thoroughly enjoy myself. When he went in to bat I'd feel very proud of him. I knew very little about the game, and made a few blunders. One was seeing him walk out from the pavilion to bat, and failing to note what happened next. I looked down for a moment to my knitting, then looked up again only to see him walking back to the pavilion. 'Oh. Tea time,' I said to my friend, and began to put away my knitting, not realizing he was out for a duck.

There was a great fuss about one game. Bill was playing for Oldham against Middleton. Their professional was the West Indian Roy Gilchrist, one of the world's great fast bowlers. He had injured quite a few players in the past with his lightning bowling. On this occasion Gilchrist's team were 183 all out. When Bill's team were 23 for 3 (injured), he thought he'd better declare, as he was next man in! We were about to go on

70

holiday the following Monday, and he wasn't going to take any chances of being injured himself. It was seen as a protest against rough play, and there was a lot of publicity at the time. League cricket always seemed to me to be a much rougher game than County or Test cricket, and today the players are all padded, and wear shields when they play against fast bowlers.

On the whole, after we were married, cricket to me meant mainly a bag full of dirty cricket flannels, shirts and sweaters — and lots of threepenny bits. In the League they had collections for scorers of a certain number of wickets. Bill nearly always came home with a collection, which meant that the milkman and the man in the paper shop became used to being paid in loose change.

The world of League cricket was very competitive when Bill was a professional cricketer. There were about twenty teams in a League, and each team would have a professional. The more money the club had, then the better paid he would be. Garfield Sobers, Sonny Ramadin, Cecil Pepper and George Tribe would come over from their home countries to play, and of course some of the English County players would also take part. Alf Gover was one, for whom Bill coached at his famous cricket school. I know Bill missed his cricket when we later moved to Brighton, but the travelling became too much. He played for Sussex second team occasionally, but after Lancashire League cricket it seemed pretty tame. I was very proud of his press cuttings, and of headlines such as: LAWTON DAMPENS SOBERS FIRE; LION-HEARTED LAWTON; NEW PROFESSIONAL THRILLS CROWD; LAWTON'S SENSATIONAL NEW LEAGUE RECORD, and of course the one when we married: LAWTON WEDS ACTRESS. Sadly, in one of the many burglaries we have suffered, all except one of Bill's cricket trophies

71

were stolen. The one which is left is a silver cricket ball with an inscribed silver plaque which says: TEN WICKETS FOR 24 RUNS. WHITEHAVEN V. HAVERICK 1955.

At the time I was rehearsing *At the Lyric* I was also playing Miss Plum, the expert in giving advice to the lovelorn in the radio series *Much-Binding-in-the-Marsh*. Several months before we were married, Bill and I had already bought a small house in London, and dizzy with impending domesticity I used to turn up at the BBC with my handbag stuffed with bits of carpet, wallpaper, and snippets of curtain material, and seek advice from Richard Murdoch and Kenneth Horne. 'I loathe that colour!' Dickie Murdoch would say, looking at one of my samples displayed for his opinion.

'Nonsense! It's lovely,' Ken would argue.

They really weren't any help at all, and it became obvious that I was much better off pleasing myself. I love creating nice surroundings, and our first home together was something very special. I wanted it to be perfect in every way for us, but so obsessed was I with being the Good Wife that on the opening night of *At the Lyric*, when Alan Melville came backstage during the show to tell me it was going well, he found me on my hands and knees in my dressing room, cutting out pelmets for the window of the spare bedroom. Alan was amazed, and used to tell everyone that story. I could never see anything strange about it at all. Once a show has started there's nothing you can do about it except keep going, and hope you reach the end without anything too awful going wrong. It's a bit like swimming the Channel. The critic who labelled me 'dear dopey Dora' somewhere about that time, could not possibly have known that there were moments during that revue when the dopey look creeping across my face stemmed from a mind divided between the dialogue on stage and the problem of what to give my husband for dinner.

I also found that I succumbed quite easily to sales talk, with the result that I found myself buying things for the house — gadgets, items which might 'come in useful', all manner of bits and pieces. People could sell me anything with some persuasive patter. I had to curb this weakness in the end, because thanks to a super salesman at a garage which looked after my car, I bought a great number of tyres. I don't just mean the ones on the car wheels, but others as well, and I had enough tyres festooning my lock-up garage to outlast the car. I needed Bill to take me in hand about this sort of thing.

Whenever he came home from one of his cricket trips, his train would arrive at Euston at about four o'clock on a Sunday morning. I organized myself beautifully so that between arriving home from the theatre on a Saturday night after the show, and going to meet Bill at the station at four in the morning, I could prepare all the vegetables for the next day, and bake enough cakes, apple pies and lemon meringue pies to feed an army. When I think about it now I realize that I can't have had any sleep on Saturday nights at all. I was so anxious to be at the station in time that I'd start off far too early, and drive through the empty streets to Euston long before the train was due. The porters got to know me, and always gave me a nice cup of tea while I waited. Then I'd drive Bill home. The next day we would start to plough through my enormous store of food, and towards the end of the day, when it became quite obvious that we were never going to eat it all, Bill often had to phone some of his cricketing friends with an SOS: 'For heaven's sake come round and help us to eat some of this food . . .'

Looking at the list of films I was in during the late

73

Forties and through the Fifties, I have little recollection of some of them. I was much in demand for cameo parts, and by the time I was thirty-seven years old I had made twenty-eight films, but had never seen my name in lights. Sometimes I pause while walking past a television set, and recognize the face and the familiar high-pitched voice. Then I realize it's some old film with me playing a waitress, a barmaid or a floozy. There was one with Sonny Tufts, and one with Ray Milland, the name of which escapes me. I met Ray Milland some years later, and he couldn't remember the film either, but he recalled me, and the song I had to sing in the film, 'I've Got a Buttonhole for Baby'. Then there was the unlikely part of Akim Tamiroff's favourite wife and member of his harem in *You Know What Sailors Are*. For some strange reason the favourite member of the harem was supposed to come from Lancashire. Nobody explained why, as far as I remember. But one thing I don't forget was working on *No Highway* with Marlene Dietrich and James Stewart. Just to see her sitting there, watching me do my little part, was sheer magic for me. Then for sheer zany humour, what could be better than a film called *Old Mother Riley Meets the Vampire*? A title to conjure with. I played the part of a maid in Bela Lugosi's household, who was being fed on liver to enrich her blood, because she was to be the next unsuspecting victim of the vampire. Richard Wattis was also in that film with me, and if we had our giggling fits it was quite legitimate, because it really was a very funny film, and most enjoyable to make. Bela Lugosi, noted for horror films and roles which chilled the blood, was absolutely charming. Dear Arthur Lucan, known for years in the variety theatre as Old Mother Riley before he ever went into films, was such a nice man, but, like so many wonderful comics, his life was full of sadness. His wife, Kitty McShane, who always played the part of his daughter on stage, was barred by then from the film studios because it was said she caused trouble. But this did not stop her from turning up briefly each day, in her Rolls Royce, to give Arthur his day's pocket money.

Miranda was a film in which Glynis Johns played the part of a mermaid, and I was in the sequel film with her, which was called *Mad About Men*. I played Glynis's friend — also a mermaid — and it was terribly exhausting because we had to spend all day wearing fish tails, which had been skilfully constructed by Messrs Dunlop (better known for tyres), and the tails were six feet long. I suppose it was thought that if they could make car tyres they would also be good at making mermaids' tails, and although they looked most realistic, those tails caused endless trouble.

On the first day of filming Glynis and I were covered with Vaseline from our waists downwards, and had to slide into the tails. It was like getting into skin-tight jeans, except that the fish tails completely disposed of our legs and feet, so that once we were inside them we were helpless and had no means of balancing. We had to be carried everywhere, and were pushed on to the set in a couple of wheelchairs. No expense had been spared at Pinewood Studios. An enormous swimming pool had been constructed into the sound stage, and filled with pretty tropical fish and fresh salmon. Nobody quite knew what was going to happen when the mermaids took to the water, but Messrs Dunlop were full of confidence that everything would be all right, so I volunteered to go in first. There was only one way it could be done, as I hadn't any legs and feet, and that was for me to be thrown in by someone else. In fact, they didn't throw me in; they thought they would tilt the wheelchair forward, and I could then slide gracefully into the pool. Perhaps the chair was tilted a little

75

too rapidly, but I was unceremoniously tipped into the water like a corpse in a burial at sea. As I went in, the fish tail shot up, and my top half went under and remained there. I couldn't regain my balance, and swallowed a lot of swimming pool, not to mention a few guppies and neon tetras, while the salmon swam around like mad, wondering what had hit them. I was terrified. Fortunately the stunt girl was already in the water, and came to the rescue, managing to get my head above the surface. I was hauled out, coughing and spluttering, and shivering with fright. Glynis Johns took one look at this dramatic scene, and promptly turned her wheelchair around, and began to propel herself back towards her dressing room at an alarming speed.

Obviously something had to be done about the fish tails. The men from Dunlop were sent for, and after much discussion about how to turn girls into mermaids they solved the problem by filling the tails with water before we slid into them, so that they were heavier than our top halves. What a messy business it was! The Vaseline had been bad enough. By the end of a long stretch of filming in the heated pool, and with the extra heat of the studio lights, the fresh salmon was not so fresh, and the other fish were nicely warmed up. The studio began to smell distinctly like a fish market. Some of the crew treated themselves to a few salmon teas, but I must say the idea didn't appeal to me at all.

With theatre and films I was doing quite well in London. Mum and Dad were very proud of my successes, but Mum's enthusiasm and her pride in my work caused a few embarrassing moments. She thought I played an unsuitable part in Alan Melville's *Simon and Laura*. It was a perfectly straight part with no laughs in it at all. All I had to do was to look nice, wearing some lovely clothes by Mark Luker, and say the lines. From

Mum's point of view her daughter was not being displayed to the best advantage. After the first night she buttonholed Binkie Beaumont, who had presented the play, and Alan Melville, and issued the challenge, 'Well, what are you going to do about Dora's part? It won't do.' Alan and Binkie were quite charming about it. Binkie pacified Mum by saying, 'Mrs Broadbent, your daughter can play anything. She's as clever as paint.' But despite this strange-sounding compliment from Binkie, and Alan's charm, obviously there was no chance that the play was going to be altered in order to exploit the comedy talents of Mrs Broadbent's daughter at the expense of the other characters. Even the press in Manchester, where we had opened before coming to London, accosted Alan Melville in defence of their local girl. 'You've crucified our Dora!' they said. Despite all this, Alan and I always remained good friends, and he wrote some wonderful revue sketches for me.

The other stars of *Simon and Laura* were Coral Browne, Roland Culver, and Ian Carmichael. Although I knew Ian very well from our revues together, Coral and Roly Culver seemed at first to be extremely remote and sophisticated. I found Coral positively frightening at the outset; she had a biting wit which terrified me. I don't think she liked me filming during the run of the play. I suppose, like Yvonne Arnaud, she thought it made me too tired to work in the evenings, and felt I should be giving all my attention to the play. But I felt fine, and at that particular time I did not seem to be suffering from overwork. This, however, was not Coral's opinion. One night I was standing in the wings next to her, waiting to go on, when she suddenly said accusingly, in that chillingly clear voice, 'You've been filming again.'

'Not today, Coral,' I replied.

'Yes, you have,' she argued. 'You can't fool me. Your

eyes are like great pools of blood on the stage.' As I was about to make my first entrance, it was not the most tactful thing to say, but I took my two 'pools of blood' on to the stage and hoped I didn't look too bad. It took me a long time to like Coral, but I do, and I think she's a wonderful actress.

The film work was still coming in. There was *Operation Bullshine* with Ronald Shiner, *The Night We Got the Bird* with Brian Rix and Ronnie Shiner, and *Carry On, Sergeant*, the first of that long-running *Carry On* series.

When the run of *Simon and Laura* came to an end I had a few days to spare before beginning rehearsals for *The Water Gypsies*. Bill and I still hadn't had a real honeymoon, and I felt in need of a break. It was summer, and Bill couldn't come away with me as he was on a cricket tour in Durham, so off I went with my understudy from *Simon and Laura* — Pauline Stroud — and her boy friend Tommy. We took the night train to Toulon to spend a while in the South of France. I had eaten some strawberries on the way, and they made me very ill. I was depressed, and began to wish I'd never gone. Anyway, I felt I was playing 'gooseberry' to Pauline and her boy friend, who would obviously much rather have been alone together, so I suddenly decided to change all my plans. I promptly returned to England and made my way to Durham to join Bill on the cricket tour.

The tour of the north-east proved to be great fun, and finished at Seaburn, on the coast. More than thirty years later I found myself in the same area again, and went into a newsagent's shop to buy a paper. The lady who owned the shop greeted me with great warmth. 'You were in here many years ago,' she told me. 'I remember you were wearing a blue knitted dress with a leather belt.' How nice to be remembered after all those years had passed, and I was amazed at the details this smiling Geordie lady had stored in her memory bank. It's a very friendly part of the world.

After the Durham tour it was back to London and rehearsals for *The Water Gypsies*, which opened in the West End in August 1955. It was written by Sir Alan Herbert, and had music by Vivian Ellis. I had the marvellous part of Lily Bell. During the first year of my marriage it seemed I had everything I could wish for — a husband, a home, and, at long last, the realisation of a dream I had cherished since leaving Oldham all those years ago — my name in lights in the West End. I had to thank *The Water Gypsies* for making that dream come true. Of course the real stars were Alan Herbert and Vivian Ellis, and on opening night, quite rightly, the big neon sign outside the theatre spelt out: A.P. HERBERT'S *THE WATER GYPSIES*.

Next day when the papers came out, the critics had all given me marvellous notices. Peter Saunders, who was presenting the show, telephoned me at home and asked, 'Can you get to the theatre early this evening? There's something I want to show you.' When I arrived he was waiting for me at the stage door of the Winter Garden Theatre (now called the New London Theatre, which isn't nearly such a nice name). Peter walked me along Drury Lane, and I still had no idea what it was he wanted to show me. He refused to say. Then as we reached the front of the theatre he said, 'Now. Look up.' I did so, and there it was in lights: DORA BRYAN in A.P. Herbert's *The Water Gypsies*. It was one of those magic moments in life that one can never capture again.

Shortly after opening, I was invited, for some reason, with Sir Alan Herbert to a Foyle's literary luncheon, and fell victim to his wicked sense of humour. I'd never been to a literary luncheon before, and hoped I wasn't going to sit next to someone I didn't know about, or who would talk a lot about books I hadn't read. I asked

Alan if he knew where I was sitting, and he replied, 'Next to Frank Cousins.'

'Who's he?' I asked, not being heavily into politics and the hierarchy of Trades Union leaders. I thought he was probably a writer.

'He's a singer,' replied Alan with a perfectly straight face.

So I sat down next to this rather serious-looking bespectacled gentleman, who seemed very pleasant, but somehow he didn't look much like a singer. Perhaps he sang in opera or something, I thought. I turned to him to make polite conversation, and said, 'How are things?'

'Oh, you know what things are like in our job,' replied Mr Cousins. 'Always busy.'

The conversation took some unlikely turns, and as I couldn't very well ask him outright who he was, because the longer we talked the more complicated it became, it took me the rest of the lunch to find out.

People not connected with the theatre sometimes have the strangest ideas of how a show is put together. When I was in rep I was sometimes asked, 'Who writes your little plays? Do you just get together on the Monday and decide what you're going to say?' I have also been asked, 'How do you know when it's your turn to speak?' Others have said, 'Oh, I could never learn all those parts. How do you do it?' I always reply, 'You'd do it if you had to. If you didn't, you'd look awfully foolish on stage, not knowing any dialogue.' I make sure I know the dialogue backwards, as the saying goes. Not always an advantage. A well-known actress was on one occasion stumbling through her lines in a Noel Coward play, and afterwards made her excuses to the author: 'But Noel, I knew it backwards in bed last night.' To which Noel icily replied, 'I'd rather you had known it forwards on stage today.'

The big nightmare of most actors and actresses is dreaming of being on stage, or even backstage in a show, and vaguely knowing what the show's about, but not actually knowing what it is they have to say. Someone keeps whisking the script away just at the last minute. Fortunately, we do wake up, just before we die of fright. Knowing the words perfectly makes me feel really secure, so that I can simply get on with my performance. In *The Water Gypsies* I was given a very complicated number to learn overnight. Alan Herbert and Vivian Ellis wanted it put into the matinée next day. It was the number 'Why Did You Call Me Lily?' and the lyric was extremely tricky. Here is just a small part of it:

> *You might have called me Merry,*
> *Or Calorie or Cool;*
> *Jolly or Jungleberry,*
> *Or Taffeta or Tulle,*
> *Or Nicotine or Columbine,*
> *Or Atom Bomb or Bubbly wine;*
> *Aspirin or Iodine,*
> *But Lily isn't me*
> *Amami, Ammonia, Bacteria, Begonia;*
> *Calypso, Calpurnia,*
> *Hydrangea or Hernia;*
> *Any name will do. .*
> *Victoria or Waterloo . . .*

It went on like this, and was quite something to learn overnight, so to be really sure of myself I resorted to an old-fashioned repertory company trick. I covered my arms with wet-white (liquid make-up), and in ball-point pen wrote most of the tricky lyrics on the inside of my arms and hands, and did the whole number with arms outstretched. Even so, I was rigid with nerves. I came offstage and said, 'I'm not doing *that* again!' But I did, and it stopped the show on the opening night.

Three months into the run of *The Water Gypsies* came the one thing needed to make my happiness complete. I found that I was going to have a baby. There was just one cloud on the horizon, and that was the task of having to break the news to the theatre management, which I dreaded having to do. The show was proving to be a huge success and was likely to settle down for a long run, so my pregnancy was, to say the very least, going to be a serious inconvenience for them. I kept putting off the day when I would have to break the news, but it was one of those things which wasn't going either to go away or become any easier. When I finally plucked up courage to drop my bombshell I was naturally very unpopular. They had made me the star of the show; they had put my name in lights, and now I was saying that within a comparatively short time I was going to have to leave the cast. They couldn't find anyone to take over from me, and the show had to close after a run of only six months, when it could have gone on for much longer. Although I was thrilled about the baby, I felt dreadfully guilty about letting down the show. It wasn't even as though I could do it quietly, because the reason for the closure had to be given to the press. One newspaper, assessing the management's potential financial loss, headlined its story: THE £20,000 BABY.

Yet in the end all that heartache and guilt was for nothing, and a new heartache took its place. My baby was born prematurely, and did not survive. There came the sense of futility and devastation which all women suffer when they lose their first baby. It seemed that the only way for me to break out of the terrible depression which gripped me was to get back to work immediately. It had already been arranged that after my baby was born I should star in a 52-week series for Granada TV called *Our Dora*. Now I wanted to start work on it straight away in order to occupy myself and keep active, leaving little time to brood. I wasn't even physically fit, and my agent tried to reason with me, but I absolutely insisted. 'I must get back to work and forget about the baby,' I said. So as a result, the whole series was brought forward, and within three weeks of leaving hospital, I was rehearsing for the TV shows.

We did the first episode 'live' from the Manchester studio of Granada Television. It went very well, but when it was over I collapsed. My agent had been right, and I had been wrong. I really was in no fit state to be working under that kind of pressure, and I should not have insisted on doing so. I had to go before a medical board, and Granada TV even sent me to a psychiatrist to prove that I was physically and mentally incapable of carrying on. Perhaps that all sounds very cold and callous on the part of the TV management, but it was for insurance purposes, and there was a great deal of money tied up in the series. As for me, I had a nervous breakdown and did not work again for nine months. I began to feel I had reached rock bottom, and was in a mood of black despair. Here was I, the actress who had always prided herself on being a trouper, a real professional, and I had left in the lurch first a theatre management and now a television company. I even began to wonder whether anyone would want to employ me again.

I completely lost confidence in myself. Frightened of meeting people, dreading pity, I avoided my friends and kept well away from the West End. I had been neither helped nor encouraged by anything the psychiatrist said. He told me that my collapse in Manchester had come about because the day I did the TV show — 26 September — was the date on which my baby should have been born if I had carried it to the full

83

term. Subconsciously, he said, this had been at the back of my mind. Doubtless he was right, but he was not telling me anything I did not know. Did he really think I was not *consciously* aware of that date? His diagnosis wasn't exactly helpful, if anything it made me feel even worse. And all the tablets I was taking did not seem to be having a beneficial effect either. How could they? I was taking sleeping pills to knock me out, and pep-up pills to wake me up again and stave off depression. I finished up in such a state of confusion that in the end I threw them all away.

In the meantime the Granada Television series went ahead without me, retitled *My Wife's Sister*, and with Eleanor Summerfield in the lead.

It was either fate or coincidence, but just before I had my breakdown, Mum and Dad had decided to come and live in London. My brother was settled in South Africa, and the dress shop Mum had opened in Oldham was doing very well, with an excellent manageress to run it. It seemed there were no longer any ties to keep my parents in Oldham, and everyone thought it would be nice for us all to be together. Mum, energetic as ever, immediately looked around for something to keep her occupied in London. She was not one for letting the grass grow under her feet, so she and Dad set about buying a small hotel in Queens Gate, South Kensington. Small it may have been by London standards, but it still cost a lot of money. Bill and I decided to sell our little house in Hillgate Place, Notting Hill, share the purchase of the hotel, and help to run it.

If I had not already suffered a nervous breakdown, Park House Hotel would have been enough to give me one, but I was kept far too busy to dwell very much upon my health. Four people, knowing nothing about the hidden traps of running a hotel, and with no experience, suddenly finding themselves in charge of a twenty-bedroom establishment, is a recipe for certain disaster. It must have been obvious to the staff as soon as we walked through the doors that we did not know the first thing about the hotel business, and they exploited the fact to the full.

When we first arrived we were confronted by a frosty-faced receptionist, who looked us up and down and sniffed, as though we were only fit to enter via the tradesmen's entrance. Our barbarous northern accents soon proved to be more than her sensitive ears could bear, and she departed for ever, leaving me to cope with the switchboard. I had never been faced with a switchboard in my life, and almost immediately there came a flood of complaints from guests who found themselves cut off in the middle of calls while I juggled with a tangle of plugs and wires, and usually succeeded in putting the wrong plugs in the wrong sockets, and pulling plugs out of other wrong sockets, all of which caused chaos. I could cope with the local calls, but trunk calls were a complete disaster, and I invariably managed to cut everybody off in mid-conversation.

Occasionally when I was walking around the hotel one guest would say to another, 'Doesn't that girl look like Dora Bryan?' I would pretend that I hadn't heard, and would move on a little quicker, before anyone decided to say anything to me.

It was difficult to say which were the worse headaches, the staff or the guests. Some of the guests were charming, of course, and among these was a lady who I believe was the widow of Arnold Bennett. She was delightful, but we tried not to encourage permanent residents because they were often very eccentric. Some of them really should have been in nursing homes. We had old ladies who were professional neurotics, and we had hypochondriacs and alcoholics. One resident was a Jehovah's Witness, who was very hot on Armageddon, and another was a Christian Scientist who was always grabbing me and trying to convert me. We had one elderly lady who was sweet, but was always getting lost. We had to keep going to collect her from chemist shops and florists. There was one woman who drank excessively, and talked even more — mostly on the telephone, so perhaps she suffered most from my inefficiency on the switchboard. She summoned my mother one day and threatened to leave the hotel immediately unless 'that wretched switchboard operator' was sacked at once.

'The switchboard operator,' replied Mum with splendid dignity, 'happens to be my daughter.'

Among the staff were five Irish chambermaids, some of whom were sent out from time to time with five-pound notes, to get them changed, and promptly disappeared for ever. One of our chefs was an ex-army cook, and if it's true that an army marches on its stomach, I can't believe that the men who used his cookhouse marched anywhere at all. His idea of cooking a rice pudding in a slow oven was to set the oven going full blast, and leave the oven door open. He cooked chickens just as they came from the poulterers, shoving them in the oven, guts and all! Our floating population of waitresses included several who — as we discovered when we checked our wine merchant's bill — must have been steadily drinking themselves to death at our expense. One by one the staff took flight, which meant that there was even less time for me to consider my health, as I had to fill in and do all manner of jobs. Both Bill and I would be up very early, and we were down in the icy cold kitchen at 7.30 each morning, helping Mum to cook breakfast. Then I would serve at table, answer the telephone (praying it wasn't a complicated call!), and as I was rushing around doing various jobs it wasn't unusual for me to meet Bill on the stairs, staggering under a load of suitcases, and trying at the same time to cope with some ridiculous demand from a fractious guest.

Our one salvation in all this turmoil was Ivor. Strictly speaking, he was the kitchen porter, but he could — and did — turn his hand to anything. When all the chambermaids walked out, Ivor remained with us and did their jobs. When the chef left, Ivor cooked, and did it much better than the original chef. When the waitress departed, it was Ivor who served at table with all the aplomb of a waiter at the Savoy. He was an absolute treasure, and remained with us long after we sold Park House Hotel, becoming our housekeeper. Several times when we were between nannies he proved himself to be perfectly capable of tackling that job too, with a combination of common sense and the occasional dip into the baby book if he was in any doubt. The invaluable Ivor has been known to cure an attack of nappy rash overnight.

We took turns in cooking at the hotel after the departure of half the staff. One evening it was the turn of Bill and myself to cook the evening meal. When seven o'clock came, everything was ready. The soup was hot, the meat was carved, just waiting to have the gravy poured on to it, to be served with the vegetables, followed by apple pie and custard. Bill and I sat in the kitchen, waiting for Ivor to shout his orders down the lift shaft. Eventually the first order came: 'Six soups, please!' We sprang to our feet and began to ladle out the soup. When all six plates were ready I loaded up the food lift, and Bill started to turn the winch to raise it. It was a very awkward lift, and instead of Ivor receiving the soup at his end of the lift, all six plates tipped over Bill. This meant a hasty clean-up, replacing the six ordered soups, and a general panic while we served up the rest of the meal. The orders came thick and fast, and we breathed a sigh of relief when it was 8.30 and all the guests had been fed. I learned so much during our time as hoteliers that I now never grumble about anything when I'm staying in a hotel. It always crosses my mind that we don't know what is going on behind the scenes, and that perhaps the proprietors might be going through a few of our experiences. It must be said that during all this time Bill was still coaching cricket at Alf Gover's school at Wandsworth, as well as helping in the hotel.

For many months I had cut myself off from my profession. All confidence gone, I had repeatedly turned down offers of work. But whatever else that awful hotel had done to us, the sheer slog of running it had driven away the last traces of my breakdown. Bill and I took ourselves off to Majorca for a holiday, and while we were there I announced, 'I'm going to accept the first job that's offered to me when we get back. I don't give a damn what it is.'

The luck which I thought had deserted me for ever suddenly returned. While we were away a cable arrived from Ronald Shiner: BE MY WIFE IN MY NEXT PRODUCTION. I wired back: YES.

Ronnie Shiner and I had known each other for years, and he was a good friend. I could not have wished for anyone better to be at my side when I took that first apprehensive step back into show business. For some reason he was as nervous as I was. The play was a comedy, *The Love Birds*, and while it can hardly be described as a smash hit, it ran well, and I look upon it with affection because it was such a help in making me regain faith in myself. It was also memorable for other reasons. Bill and I realized that we wanted our own home again, so we bought a house in Barnes, while Mum and Dad bought a flatlet house in Onslow Gardens. That marked the end of our hotel venture. The other landmark was that during the run of *The Love Birds* I discovered I was pregnant again. I was thrilled, but then came that familiar agony about how I was going to break the news to the management. It seemed that my pregnancies were never theatrically convenient. But this time I need not have worried. Emile Littler, who had put on the show, was kindly, and very family-minded. He was as thrilled as we were.

When we moved to Barnes we found the most wonderful handyman in the form of a chap called Bill Sackett. He did so many odd jobs for us, and we wanted to pay him by the hour. Mr Sackett declined with scrupulous honesty. 'I can't charge you by the hour because I'm a slow worker,' he said. Slow worker or not, Bill Sackett became almost one of the family. He was a man of interesting opinions, often expressed in the funniest ways. When I had made my floor-to-ceiling, plush velvet curtains for our large Georgian windows, I drew them on their cord, swishing them across for him to see. He stood quietly for a moment, lost in admiration. 'Oh, Dora,' he breathed, 'it's just like the Gaumont.'

Bill Sackett and his wife became caretakers at Mum and Dad's flatlet house, and would chauffeur me to and from the theatre when asked.

I was absolutely determined that nothing would go wrong with this pregnancy, and that I would keep this baby at all costs. I stayed in bed all day, and only got up at five o'clock before driving to the theatre. I really looked after myself, and was five months pregnant when I left the show. In the play I wore a pretty red double-breasted suit with a pleated skirt, and during the run it was let out so many times as I expanded that it finished up as a single-breasted suit with a straight skirt.

Two months after leaving the play I had a second

premature baby, who survived only a few days. I was devastated, and my first thought was that I had continued to work too far into my pregnancy. But looking back, I believed I was healthier during the five months in which I worked than I was in the last two months at home as a housewife, busying myself with cooking, cleaning and decorating. Whatever the reason for losing this second baby, I made up my mind that I was not going to have another breakdown. Bill was wonderful. The loss of this baby had been terrible for him too, and I suppose he simply didn't know what to say when he came to see me in Queen Charlotte's Hospital. He walked into my room, desperately wanting to cheer me up, and not quite knowing how to go about it. His words of consolation will remain with me for ever . . . 'Never mind. At least the garden will be lovely next summer. I've had two tons of manure delivered today.'

One of the specialists came in to see me before I left the hospital. 'Have you ever thought of adoption, Mrs Lawton?' he asked. My heart sank. Did that mean that there was no chance of having children of my own? My face must have reflected my feelings, because he went on, 'I'm not saying that you can't have children of your own eventually, but frankly, you're not an easy case, and we can't guarantee that you'll ever be able to carry a child to the full term. I'm a great fan of yours, you know, and I'd like to see you go back to the stage for a couple of years. Then try again. If you had an adopted child, I'm sure it would help you.'

That afternoon I had a long talk with the lady almoner about adoption. It wasn't something one could suddenly decide upon. Both Bill and I had to make the decision, and when the almoner left I spent a long time thinking about it. There were so many aspects to consider. I couldn't wait for Bill to come and visit me after he finished at the cricket school that evening.

3. In the *Lyric Revue*.

4. In *The Cure for Love* with Robert Donat.

5. Wedding day, 1954.

6. With Akim Tamiroff and Donald Sinden in *You Know What Sailors Are*.

7. Glynis Johns and me in *Mad about Men*, with our tails on.

8. Our first house in Brighton.

When he arrived he came in bearing a bottle of champagne. Well, at least it was better than a load of manure, and Sister had told him the previous evening that a bottle of bubbly was just what I needed. It could not have been more appropriate as it happened.

'The specialist had a talk with me today,' I began, 'and guess what he talked about? He suggested that we might like to adopt a baby.' I waited for the reaction, and then went on, 'But we want our own baby . . . don't we?'

I don't know what sort of response I expected, but Bill did not bat an eyelid. 'Oh, I don't know,' he replied. 'If you get one young enough I suppose it's like having one of your own, without all the problems you've had of having to leave shows and let managements down.'

He was half joking, but he knew the worries and guilt feelings I had suffered over this, and I could see that the idea of adoption did not come as a shock to him, nor did he turn it down out of hand. We talked about it a bit more, and before Bill left we were using the bottle of champagne to celebrate our decision. We were going to adopt a baby. After Bill had gone I couldn't sleep for excitement. I was quite prepared to go and collect a baby the next morning, but of course it wasn't going to be as easy as all that.

Each time my babies had died, I had wept on Mum's shoulder, asking why it should have happened to us, and she had said, 'Dora, God has a reason for everything. He works in strange and wonderful ways.' I know now just what she meant. If we hadn't lost our two babies we would never have been in a position to adopt Daniel and Georgina, two children who were definitely meant to belong to us. They both came to us at the age of six weeks, and from the moment you start to take care of an adopted baby, it is yours. I find it very hard to understand all this talk about 'your own flesh

and blood'. I love my husband, but he is not, bio-
logically, my own flesh and blood. It makes no difference, and loving an adopted baby is the same as loving
your own.

Our first step along the long road of the adoption
process was to decide whom to approach. We chose the
Church of England Adoption Society, and were sent an
alarmingly detailed questionnaire to complete. Under
the heading of 'Hobbies' I wrote 'cooking' for me and
'tropical fish' for Bill, in the hope of sounding suitably
conventional and domestic, if that was the sort of thing
they wanted. Under 'Occupations' I'd already written
'actress' and 'professional cricketer', and that was quite
enough eccentricity for one application form! We had
to produce medical certificates giving us a clean bill of
health, and a letter from my specialist saying he
thought it essential for me to have a baby to look after,
to satisfy my maternal instincts. To prove that we were
happily married we had to provide references from
people who had known us for years. Every one of these
was scrupulously followed up — not merely by letter,
but by personal visits.

Then came a period of total silence. I went back to
work in a new revue. Three months passed before we
heard that our application had been accepted in principle, and we would be receiving a visit from the
Society's adoption officer. It all sounded formidable,
and when the day came, Bill took the afternoon off
work so that he was at home to be inspected. We were
very nervous, worrying about the kind of impression
we would make. It seemed to us that anyone seeking an
ordinary, conventional background for a child must
place an actress and a cricketer pretty low down on the
list of desirable parents. We could only hope for the
best. I took the precaution of removing the bottles of
drink from the sideboard, just in case they gave the

impression that we were drunkards. Then on second thoughts I left out the sherry decanter, as a symbol of genteel hospitality. Just as the doorbell rang I spotted some aspirins on the mantelpiece. I hid them under a cushion in case they gave the impression that we were a house of neurotics.

We need not have worried. 'Adoption Officer' is a forbidding title, but nobody could have been less austere than Mrs Biggs, an attractive middle-aged woman with a great sense of humour. If she recognized me as Dora Bryan she never revealed it. We were just Mr and Mrs Lawton, an ordinary couple who wanted one of her beloved babies. In the three hours she spent with us she had to find out all about us, and what kind of life we could offer a child. I could see that Bill was making a good impression by just being himself and saying very little. Nervousness was taking its toll of me and making me talk far too much. I could feel myself babbling away, and there was nothing I could do about it. Bill was quite unruffled when Mrs Biggs suddenly asked, 'Would you prefer a boy or a girl, Mr Lawton?' His reply was the classic understatement of all time. 'Oh, anything's all right by me,' he said, just as though he'd been asked whether he liked his tea weak or strong. But Mrs Biggs understood him, and knew perfectly well that he was not nearly as nonchalant as he sounded. This was just as important to him as it was to me.

We passed our test after Mrs Biggs had visited certain friends of ours to find out more about our private lives. Then started another long period of waiting. I was lucky, because unlike some 'expectant mothers' in the same situation, I was working and had plenty to occupy my mind. I was starring in *Living for Pleasure*, with Daniel Massey, Patience Collier, and George Rose, now a successful star in New York. I had lots of good numbers and sketches, among them a tart-with-a-heart-of-gold song 'No Better Than She Should Be', and the spoof ballet sketch based on *Spectre de la Rose*. There was also a sketch called 'Daphne', in which Patience Collier and I sat in a tea shop talking about our 'dear' friend Daphne, whom we reduced to pulp. At the end of the sketch, supposedly seeing Daphne in the distance, we both said as one voice, 'Daphne darling! We were just talking about you.' One summer evening, during this sketch, a large Red Admiral butterfly, attracted by the stage spotlight, dive-bombed us as we sat at the table. The audience was mesmerized, and so were we. I don't like flying fluttery things at the best of times. It eventually landed on a tea cup. Patience gently picked it up without a word, put it in her handbag, and we carried on with the sketch. I was full of admiration. After the show Patience drove to Regent's Park and gave our scene-stealer its freedom.

Still waiting for our baby, we worried about my father, whose health had not been very good towards the end of our hotel venture. When Mum and Dad moved out, they bought Number 23 Onslow Gardens, in South Kensington, which was a flatlet house, with a charming ground-floor flat, which they kept for themselves. Shortly after their move it was revealed that my father had cancer and only six months to live. My mother nursed him at home throughout his illness. It was during the run of *Living for Pleasure*, and I would call on them on my way to the Garrick Theatre, and again on my way home. It was a dreadful time for everyone, because we were all trying to keep secret the seriousness of Dad's illness, and we all knew the truth. He knew he was dying, and took me into his confidence, with strict instructions that I was not to let Mum know. But of course she knew all the time, and insisted

I said nothing to Dad. So there we all were, playing a sad game of subterfuge, each trying to be brave and optimistic when we knew it was to no avail. Nobody wants to see a loved parent suffering the pain of cancer, and despite the inevitable sadness when death finally comes, it is a sadness tempered with relief that the bad time is over.

Our wait for the adoption went on. The adoption officers are highly qualified people who know exactly what they are doing. While the delays may seem interminable to the waiting parents, they add up to time well spent in finding a child who is going to fit perfectly into the new home background. How can such an important task be hurried? In our case the waiting was for seven months, but having already waited so long for a baby, it seemed endless.

One morning, I was having a cup of tea in bed, and reading the morning mail. I slit open a typed envelope, read the letter inside it, and suddenly let out a wild yell. 'Bill! He's here!'

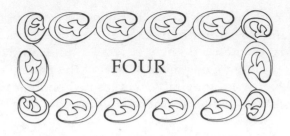

FOUR

'WE HAVE A LITTLE BOY WE WOULD LIKE TO INTRODUCE
TO you,' were the first magic words in that letter. 'He is
five weeks old, fair with blue eyes, and a real boy even
at this early age . . .' Then followed a description of his
very young parents, and enclosed was a medical report.
We were asked to telephone the adoption society and
make an appointment to see Mrs Biggs and view the
baby.

I simply don't remember doing the show that night. I
had promised to go on afterwards to appear in a charity
concert at Sutton, in Surrey, in aid of Cancer Research,
so it was 3.30 in the morning before I reached home. As
our appointment to see the baby was at 9.30, and
neither of us felt like sleeping, we decided it wasn't
worth going to bed. For the rest of the night I wandered
in and out of the newly decorated nursery, making sure
that everything was ready for the new occupant, from
nappy pins to teddy bears. We discussed where he
would go to school, what sort of job he would do when
he grew up, and Bill was very concerned about which
cricket team he would play for.

We arrived at the babies' home on the dot of 9.30,

and met Mrs Biggs, who left us for a moment in the matron's sitting room while she went for the baby. She reappeared with what seemed nothing more than a bundle of shawls, which she placed on my lap.

'I'll leave him with you for as long as you like,' she said. 'Half an hour, or an hour if you like. I don't mind. When you've made your decision just let me know. I'll be in the next room.'

I clutched the bundle and wondered what to do next. The baby was all huddled up in his shawl, and I couldn't even see his face. I had never held such a small baby, and wasn't at all sure how to do it properly. Bill was staring fixedly at my armful, and presumably could see more of it than I could. 'What does he look like?' I asked.

My husband is never a man to waste words. Brief and to the point, that's Bill. 'He's all right,' he replied. 'Put him in his carry-cot and let's take him home.'

That seemed like indecent haste, and I was a bit shocked. 'But we can't cart him away just like that,' I demurred. 'We're supposed to be making up our minds.' Mrs Biggs had said 'half an hour, or even an hour', and here we were planning to rush him home after about five minutes.

'Well there's no point in sitting here for half an hour just staring at him,' said the ever practical Bill.

'Here. You hold him,' I said, and handed over the red-faced bundle to Bill so that I could have a good look at him for the first time. He began to cry when I gave him to Bill, and when I took him back again he stopped immediately. That settled it. This baby was definitely ours.

'All right,' I said. 'Go and find Mrs Biggs, and I'll put him in his carry-cot.'

When Bill returned with Mrs Biggs the baby was fast asleep. After signing a few papers and collecting a tin of

97

dried milk, two brand-new parents very carefully stowed their baby into the car and proudly drove him home.

I had seen my last baby before he died, and was full of wonderment at him, but it was nothing to the thrill I felt on seeing our newly adopted son Daniel, fast asleep and secure in our nursery on his first night in our care. We named him after Daniel Massey, whom I was working with at the time. We loved the name, and it suited our little baby. I prayed very hard that night, not just for Bill and myself and our baby, but for Daniel's mother, who had just parted from him that morning. How was she feeling, I wondered. Although adopting parents never meet the natural mothers, I just knew that the mothers of Daniel and Georgina (whom we adopted later), must have been nice girls to have had such lovely children. Some people say, 'Aren't you wonderful to take an unwanted child into your home?' But these children aren't unwanted. Who knows, the natural mothers probably wanted their babies very badly, but in those days it was more difficult to face up to being an unmarried mother. And if only people knew just how many couples want them. Some couples are on the waiting lists for years, and we were the lucky ones, to have been given all the happiness the children have brought us.

The three-month waiting period which follows the day when the child is taken into your home is the worst part of the whole adoption procedure. You have your baby at last, and love him dearly, but yet you know that there is always just a chance, however remote it may be, that something can go wrong before the courts make him legally yours. This is an agonizing time for all adopting parents.

When Daniel arrived I was just about to start filming *Desert Mice*, with Sid James, Alfred Marks, Liz Fraser and Irene Handl. I took Daniel along to the studio every day in his carry-cot, and our nanny came too. I just couldn't bear to let him out of my sight. It was essential to engage the services of a nanny for him while I was away at the theatre, and I'm all for nannies if the right one can be found. I employed five before I found her, and despaired about ever discovering the perfect one.

Our first nanny, Anna, was a wonderful elderly Irishwoman. When I engaged her she had grey hair, but when she eventually arrived to start her new job for some reason she had dyed her hair flame red, which was a bit disconcerting. Actress Irene Handl, having encountered Anna at the studios, didn't take to her at all. After voicing her doubts Irene added, 'And I don't think Daniel's going to like waking up in the middle of the night and seeing all that red hair!' Another idiosyncrasy of Anna's was that she appeared to have a fund of very tall stories. She told us all about her castle back home in Ireland, and how she had been used to better things, but had fallen upon hard times and had been forced to sell it. We didn't believe a word of all this Irish blarney, but just smiled benignly. Then we went on holiday to Ireland, taking Anna with us, of course. She was thrilled to be going back home, and promised to take us to see her castle. We said that would be very nice, and kept on smiling. But sure and begorrah, all Anna's magnificent fairy stories turned out to be true! She took us to visit the lovely castle she had told us so much about, and we were amazed and impressed that our slightly eccentric nanny was warmly welcomed at the stately home, treated with great respect, and addressed as 'Madam'. The new owner was away at the time, so we had a conducted tour of the place, and looked upon our Anna in a very different light after the holiday.

But even this revelation could not disguise the fact

that she was just a bit dotty, although she could be interesting to talk to and I would have liked to keep her on. I never had any proof, but I was secretly convinced that she had a wooden leg. One of her legs never seemed to bend, but as both legs were encased in heavy black stockings it was difficult to tell, and this was one story she never enlarged upon. My suspicions were supported by the fact that she always came downstairs backwards, even when she was carrying things, which used to terrify the life out of me, but I thought perhaps people with artificial legs found this mode of descent a bit easier, although I couldn't logically work out why that should be. The other funny thing was that Bill kept losing his underwear, and it was some time before we discovered that Anna was making a habit of borrowing it. She was ill on one occasion, and there she was in bed clad in Bill's vest and Y-fronts.

The trouble with Anna was that she really wanted to be *my* nanny, and hadn't the requisite patience for dealing with a very young child. Eventually we found Sheila, and of course had the ever faithful Ivor from our hotel, who acted as sort of under-nanny, and helped me on Sheila's days off. By the time I had added two more children to the household during the next few years, I think I was fully qualified to write a book entitled *Nannies I Have Known*.

I had always loved Brighton from my touring days. Whenever I was given my tour list for a pre-London tour, such as Liverpool, Leeds, Manchester, Newcastle, if Brighton was on the list it was a week to treasure. We had driven to Brighton one hot sunny Sunday, with Daniel in his carry-cot, Sambo the poodle, and nanny Anna in full uniform, with the red hair topped by headdress, which she loved. We sat on the pebbles on the beach and thought how wonderful it would be to live there. That was it.

100

We happened to see a flat to let on the seafront, but the landlord said, 'No dogs or children.' Why is it that something like that makes you even more keen? The next day I was rehearsing with Brian Rix for a TV farce. It was Bill's day off, so he drove down to Brighton again and went flat-hunting. He telephoned me at rehearsal and said he'd found a house. He hadn't seen it, but the agent had made an appointment for us to view that evening. I caught the train, and off we went to see it.

The house came as quite a shock. It was a charming five-bedroomed house with so much character, tucked away up a side street, just off the seafront. We sat in the quaint sitting room, which had a verandah overlooking the garden and said, 'We'll have it.'

'Don't you want to see the rest of it?' asked the owners, surprised at the instant decision.

So we had a quick guided trip around the bedrooms. But there was more. The owner opened a door on the ground floor, which was an extension to the house, and there was an enormous dining-room with tables laid for forty people. We had bought a hotel! But I didn't care. I knew we must have it and turn it into a home. It was very old, and had originally been a two-bedroomed cottage with a lot of land. Over the years it had developed into a five-bedroomed house with a much smaller piece of land. The owners wanted to sell it as a going concern, down to the last hot water bottle, and thought we were quite crazy when we said we just wanted to live in it. We didn't want the contents, but if we wanted the place at all, then we had to take it on the owners' terms, complete with furniture and hotel trappings. We wanted the place so much that we agreed to do so.

Back in London that night, I couldn't sleep. Suddenly the purchase of a hotel seemed like a nightmare. What were we going to do with all that furniture, which wasn't our taste at all, to say nothing of all those spare beds, wardrobes, cruets, and water jugs?

There's one thing to be said about Bill, and that is that if he's worried about anything he never lets it disturb his sleep. I decided to disturb it, so I shook him and said, 'Bill, are we short of money?' That's a pretty good question to fire at someone in the middle of the night. Bill, dragged reluctantly into wakefulness, muttered non-committally, 'Well, no more than usual.'

'So why don't we let this house furnished, with all that hotel stuff in it, and take all our nice furniture down to Brighton with us? Just swap it over.'

'Mmm. Yes. If you like. I suppose so.'

So that was decided. Bill promptly went straight back to sleep. I felt much better about things, and did the same.

On moving day, our friendly removal man, Ted, came with his wife. We always had Ted to move us. He and his wagon had done all our moves, but the trouble was that our chattels had gradually outgrown his wagon, and this was to be a double move — a complete change-over of furniture. The London stuff was going to Brighton, and the contents of the Brighton hotel were coming to London. Ted's wife did the packing. I can't bear to see houses being packed up, and have always loved something about every home we've lived in. I went off with Daniel for a long walk while everyone else got on with the move. When the wagon was loaded it took off for Brighton, while the family and the animals followed by car.

When we arrived at our new Brighton home we were horrified to find that the twenty-five-foot dining-room was still set out for forty people! We had been relying upon the spacious dining-room to unload our London furniture while we reshuffled everything, so that Ted could take the stuff back to the London house. We started by clearing all the tables, emptying the water jugs, and stacking everything away so that we could unload. It became obvious that we were not going to accomplish everything in one day, so Ted and his wife stayed the night. At least all the beds were made up, and soap and towels laid out everywhere, so we were able to offer them a choice of rooms. Next day we loaded the wagon to go back to London. Ted's wife acquired a great collection of cruets and water jugs for her own home, and for months afterwards we kept the local church bazaars supplied with teapots, gravy boats and vegetable dishes. But not even a white elephant stall could offer much help in disposing of twenty china chamber pots. They hung around for quite some time.

It was a fascinating house, and the previous owners had told us it had an interesting history. They said it had once belonged to a European king who had lived on the promenade, and it had been the home of his major domo. The horses had been stabled in the back garden. It's always pleasant to own a house with a history, and I was curious to know more, so I went along to the town hall to check out the details. Any oneupmanship about owning a historic house evaporated when I discovered the truth. So much for the yarn about the European king and his household. The real story was that the house was built in 1805 by a baker, who owned a windmill at Rottingdean. So the Lawton domain, far from being a former royal residence, was distinctly middle class. Other drawbacks gradually came to light. For example, the man who came to read the gas meters could never find them, and I spent a lot of time, by trial and error, working out the shortest route to the kitchen. Bill's Mum, when she came to stay with us, wouldn't leave a room unless someone went with her to make certain she got back again. She'd been lost too many times to walk around the house alone.

103

We were in a terrible muddle at first, and hoped none of our friends would drop in before we had put the place straight. There seemed to be so much to do. But on our first Sunday there the doorbell rang, and I wondered who on earth it was going to be. On the step stood our good friend, radio and TV celebrity Gilbert Harding. In one hand he carried an enormous bouquet of flowers, and in the other hand the most useful thing he could have brought to strangers in a new town. It was a list of names, addresses, and telephone numbers of a doctor, dentist, vet, car hire firm, off-licence, and dry cleaners. A most thoughtful thing to do, and so typical of Gilbert, who could be such an abrasive personality on TV and radio, yet was such a kind soul in private life. His death greatly saddened me.

It was our first Easter in the house, and we were sitting watching television when we heard some strange voices in the hall. . .

'Oh, look! It's all been decorated. Isn't that nice? You go on up to your room, Mother, and I'll see about getting you a hot water bottle and a nice cup of tea.'

We could hardly believe it. When we went to investigate we found a family who had travelled all the way from Workington for their annual holiday at the hotel. They didn't know it had been sold, and nobody had thought to cancel their bookings. There was embarrassment all round, and I felt so sorry for them that I wanted to put them up, but Bill discreetly squashed that idea and found them rooms in a hotel round the corner.

Living in Brighton while working in London meant catching a late night train home. I needed a car to wait for me at the stage door, to take me to Victoria station. The obliging Mr Sackett, our odd job man from Barnes, volunteered. He had a rather battered, but very reliable car, and every night he waited for me, wearing his cloth cap, and invariably rolling a cigarette. He whisked me to the station in his old banger, and looked after me extremely well. Life didn't always seem like the glamorous existence of a West End star, when there were family crises to worry about, and the main thing was to give a good performance, and then get home quickly to deal with the other side of Dora Bryan — the wife and the mother, which was always of enormous concern to me. Later, when I took over from Mary Martin in *Hello, Dolly!* at Drury Lane in 1865, producer Binkie Beaumont thought I should live up to the status of a leading lady, so he arranged for a hired car to pick me up at the stage door each night, with an elegant grey-uniformed chauffeuse. The driving duties were alternated by Mary and Veronica, two frightfully nice girls, who performed the same job as our Mr Sackett had done. In fact they did even more, because they didn't mind popping into the pub opposite the stage door after the evening performance and calling out, 'Miss Bryan! Your car!' I don't think Mary Martin ever had that kind of service.

When I first moved to Brighton I wondered how on earth I was going to spend two hours a day on a train, but I soon discovered it was a wonderful place to learn lines, and nobody minded if you said, 'Hello. Yes, I'm fine, thanks, but don't come and talk to me because I'm studying lines.' There were so many theatrical people on the train that everyone understood. It was like a travelling theatre club in those magic days of the Brighton Belle, the pride and joy of Southern Railway. Each Pullman coach had its own name. There was Doris, Hazel, Audrey, Vera, Gwen, and Mona. The dining car had full waiter service, with starched white tablecloths, and champagne on ice always at the ready. The food was excellent, whether you wanted a Welsh rarebit, bacon and egg, salad, or a breakfast of kippers. Sir Laurence Olivier was desperately upset when breakfast kippers were removed from the menu. He even organized a petition which we all signed, and they were put back on again. I don't really like kippers very much, but out of loyalty to Larry I forced myself to eat them occasionally.

The atmosphere on the Brighton Belle was warm and friendly, and the air full of mouth-watering smells. It could be relied upon, day after day, to get all the South Coast theatre people up to London at 8.35 a.m. in time for rehearsals, and back at 7 p.m. from Victoria. When working in London shows we all travelled up on the 5.45 p.m. from Brighton, and came back on the 11 o'clock run, after the show. The journey was always great fun, and how could it fail to be with such travelling companions? The passenger list read like *Who's Who in the Theatre* . . . Alan Melville, the Crazy Gang, Brenda Bruce, Gilbert Harding, Max Miller, Paul Scofield, Valentine Dyall, Flora Robson, Julia Foster, Coral Browne, the Oliviers . . . everyone talking shop. Champagne flowed, and the stories were always greatly embellished. I learnt all my scripts on the train, but had to have a lot of self-discipline to force myself to sit alone when I'd much rather have chatted with my friends.

Now the Brighton journey isn't nearly so much fun. The Brighton Belle is no more. She was pensioned off at forty years of age, and so many of the theatrical personalities of the old days have either died or moved away. The glamour has gone. One is now faced with a rather scruffy buffet car, plastic cups, plastic spoons, paper plates, and instant tea and coffee served with processed milk in those maddening little containers which spurt in all directions when you open them. But on the plus side it has to be said that the Inter-City trains have improved, and I can now travel from London to Manchester in two and a half hours, a great difference from those long journeys I used to make more than forty years ago for a brief weekend with

Mum and Dad. I often look back and think how far we have travelled (not only by British Rail), towards the 'anything goes' society.

. . . A few weeks after Daniel's first birthday I was filming *The Night We Got the Bird* at Shepperton Studios, with Brian Rix and Ronnie Shiner. I'd been given two tickets for the West End musical *Flower Drum Song*. I phoned Mum from the studios to see if she would like to come with me, but the caretaker at Onslow Gardens said she'd already left for Brighton, for her usual weekend with us. Obviously she would not want to come back to London again, so I phoned Bill, suggesting he came to town and met me. He and I went to the show, and returned on the late train. Our housekeeper had gone home to Liverpool for the weekend, so I looked in on Daniel, and on Mum, who was asleep, and went to bed. Next morning I couldn't understand why Mum wasn't around. She was always an early riser. I went into her bedroom and she seemed to be fast asleep, but I noticed a slight trickle of saliva at the side of her mouth. I fetched Bill, who insisted that she was just asleep, but somehow I felt there was something dreadfully wrong. Having lived in Brighton only a short time, we had few close friends, but I knew the vicar, and called him. He telephoned a doctor, who examined Mum and informed us that she had had a cerebral haemorrhage and must not be moved. A specialist was sent for, who confirmed the diagnosis. Two nurses — a day nurse and a night nurse — cared for her round the clock. It was a nightmare. I couldn't carry on with the film, and stayed by her side, hoping for a miracle. Brian Rix was wonderfully understanding about it. This all happened on a Saturday morning, and by the following Wednesday there seemed to be some sign of improvement in Mum's condition. I was with her when Bill came into the room to say Brian Rix was on the phone for me, asking how things were, and hoping I might manage to get to the studios. Mummy squeezed my hand, as if she understood and wanted me to go back to work.

Brian and the film crew had done as much filming as they could without me, and as the nurse also said she thought Mum had improved, I decided to go back to work, after extracting a promise from Brian that a car would be standing by to whisk me back to Brighton if necessary. But by the following Saturday morning Mummy had drifted into a deeper coma, and she slipped away . . . I had no faith at all at that time. I had lost my wonderful Mum, and my best friend. Nobody has ever taken her place. I remembered all our long talks; the pride and love I had for her, and she for me. I had terrible feelings of guilt for years afterwards that if only I had phoned her earlier to invite her to go to *Flower Drum Song* she might not have had that stroke. But now I know I shall see her again one day, and that she has been at peace with Dad all these years. On the day we thought there was some improvement in her condition the night nurse had asked me who Albert was. 'He was my dad,' I told her.

'Then that accounts for it,' said the nurse, and told me that Mum had become very restless at one stage, and had said, quite clearly, 'I can't see Albert now. He's gone again.' Maybe in her deep coma she had been with him, and he had disappeared as she recovered consciousness.

I was sorry Daniel hadn't a granny any more, but he was too young to understand. Mum made his first birthday cake, and her death came only a few weeks later.

Although we wanted to adopt a little girl, we also wanted Daniel to have his full share of love and affection before we did so, and it was some months before we again applied to the adoption society. Once more we had to go through the whole procedure of medical examinations and interviews, and we were placed on the waiting list. I thought it would take longer to get a girl than a boy. For some reason they seemed to be more in demand, but seven months later we found ourselves back at the babies' home with our Mrs B. We saw our baby girl when she was ten days old, but we couldn't have her for six weeks.

'I'm not sure whether you're going to like her,' said Mrs Biggs. 'There's a bit of a drawback.'

We waited anxiously, wondering what on earth it could be. She returned, carrying that now familiar bundle. 'Look,' she said, pulling back the shawl. 'Big feet!'

They didn't look big to me, and she was such a beautiful baby. Nigel Green, an actor friend of ours, said when he first saw her asleep, 'That's no baby. That's an angel.' I had already decided she was going to be called Georgina, after my mother, and when she was safely tucked up in the nursery with Daniel, we began to feel that we really had a family. Daniel thought that this angelic baby was specially for him, and he insisted upon climbing into the cot with her, or dragging her across the floor. She was such a delightfully placid child that she put up with it all. At the time Georgina joined our family I was working on a TV series with Pete Murray called *Happy Ever After*.

About this time I was asked to do a big Christmas revue in Manchester with the comedian Al Read. I wasn't sure how I would fit into that, with my intimate revue style and material, but Richard Hurran told me I was to do one or two of my sketches, and then have my own spot. The only spot I had experienced was a pimple, and I hadn't a clue what he was talking about, which may seem strange for someone of my stage experience. 'What's that?' I asked blankly.

He looked at me equally blankly. 'You do about ten minutes on your own,' he explained, as though he was talking to a backward child. 'A few jokes, and then you finish with a song.'

Me? Telling jokes? I had only ever spoken words on stage which had been written by playwrights and script-writers, and I certainly did not see myself in the role of a stand-up comic, perhaps having to improvise. But Leslie Bricusse, now famous for *Doctor Dolittle* and *Stop the World, I Want To Get Off*, was approached. He wrote ten very funny minutes for me, plus a song, 'Today to be a Star'. That was my 'spot'. It was thrilling to be carried on stage in a blue tulle and sequin dress by two boy dancers, sing my song, and face a large audience in a spotlight. Then I would do my patter and get laughs. I could slip in a few relevant jokes as well. I did enjoy myself. I was lucky; it was a wonderful show, and Al Read is a very funny man. There was a speciality act called the Piero Brothers, the Tiller Girls were in the show, and there was lots of spectacular glamour. Such a contrast from the intimate revues I had done. It was hard work, twice nightly and three shows on a Satur-day. We had a swimming pool on stage to close the first half of the show. It was the one used in the West End musical *Wish You Were Here*, and Al Read and I had to parade around it as bathing beauties, 'Miss Oldham' and 'Miss Ashton-under-Lyne'. Of course we both finished up being pushed in the pool. To do this twice nightly and three times on a Saturday during the winter was a bit much, so I soon developed an allergy to chlorine, and organized myself a doctor's note. Anyway, I needed to save myself for my 'spot'.

From the material provided for me for this show I then had the basis of a very good act, to which I gradually added more songs and routines. It was a good training for my first cabaret date, which came some years later at the Marimba Club in Middlesbrough. I had been asked to do cabaret at the Savoy Hotel in London, and thought I'd better try out my act first as far as possible from the sophisticated West End. With Bill and Geoffrey Braun, my pianist, I arrived in Middlesbrough on a Sunday afternoon, and it really isn't the most cheerful of destinations to reach on the Sabbath, nor did it look as though it could possibly boast anything so exotic as an establishment called the Marimba Club, with all its implied glamour. It sounded like a cross between Las Vegas and the Caribbean, so I was a little put off and disconcerted when we were directed to what looked for all the world like a derelict building, despite the fact that the name was up on the outside. Inside, the smell of stale beer and old cigarette smoke was all very depressing. I thought perhaps it wasn't a good idea to have agreed to become a cabaret artist. I stood there, and then a man who looked as though he'd just walked off a building site came up to me and welcomed me to his club. It all boded ill, but I rose above it and asked him if I could meet the musical director so that I could give him my set of band parts — which were brand new, incidentally. I think that must have been the first joke I made in Middlesbrough that day, as the band couldn't read a note of the music I'd brought with me. My pianist, Geoffrey Braun, earned every penny of his fee that week, as he made his piano sound like ten men playing.

I opened on the Sunday night. It cost the customers five shillings to get in, and there was a queue right round the building. Savoy Hotel, here I come, I thought. The next night — Monday — I wondered what on earth had happened. Someone should have told me that no one goes out on a Monday night in Middlesbrough — well, not to the Marimba Club, and not to see

111

Dora Bryan! There were just two men sitting with a bottle of Asti Spumante in a bucket, two waiters behind the bar, the old man on the spotlight, and me in my sequins doing exactly the same routine that had brought the house down the previous night. I cried all the way to the dressing room. The old man on the spotlight said as I rushed past him, 'You weren't so good as last night, Dora.' I could have hit him. But by Friday the place was packed again, and my confidence was restored. I also learned that a good pianist like Geoffrey is more important than all the band parts.

Some musicians can play mean tricks at times. I do understand that they must get very bored sitting down there in the orchestra pit night after night, and after a twelve-week season at somewhere like Great Yarmouth, playing the same old songs, they must be desperate for some diversion. When I did a season at Great Yarmouth I ended my act with the lovely song, 'He's Just My Bill' from *Show Boat*, and at the end of the summer season my band parts were returned to me. They were covered with tea and beer stains, and with a few deft strokes of their pencils the musicians had converted the word 'Bill' into 'Balls'. It was interesting to learn how they had been filling in their spare moments down there in the orchestra pit, but I hoped it wasn't a reflection on my rendering of that song.

Another cabaret date on a par with the one at Middlesbrough was at Mablethorpe in Lincolnshire. It was for one show on a Sunday night, and for rather a lot of money. Geoffrey, unfortunately, was ill at the last minute, so I had to pick up another pianist in London on the drive from Brighton to Mablethorpe. Bill was driving, so at least the new pianist and I could rehearse in the car. It was quite a drive, and Mablethorpe wasn't very well signposted. We were going down what seemed like a deserted lane, leading to No Man's Land

112

with rock shops and ice cream stalls on either side. It was Sunday afternoon. Bill then informed us that he was lost. I wound down the window and accosted the only passer-by, asking if he could tell us the way to Mablethorpe. 'This is it,' he replied. Facing us on No Man's Land was a deserted beach, and a long shed on the sand, with a notice at one end saying WOMEN, and at the other end MEN. I wondered where the theatre could be. 'Could you tell us where the Floral Hall is, please?' I inquired further. 'That's it. There.' He pointed to it.

Yes, it was the shed. Oh dear, what would my mum have said if she was alive? We somehow parked the car on the sand, and carried in the sequins and feathers, and my music. Inside the shed was bedlam. A rock group was rehearsing in one corner, and some disco dancers in another, while a lot of men were trying to get the legs on a white grand piano, which I was told was for me. Everyone was very friendly, but as there was no hope of a rehearsal in all the chaos, I realized it was all in the lap of the gods, and a rest and a good pray would do me more good than anything. So we went to the hotel that had been booked for us, and tried to relax. We went back at nine o'clock to find that what had looked like a disaster had turned into a triumph. Jolly people in evening dress were queuing round the building, and the inside had been transformed into a smart nightclub — red tablecloths, candlelight, champagne buckets, flowers, waiters and waitresses . . . We had a wonderful evening with wonderful people.

I was at home in Brighton one day, just before doing a summer season in Bournemouth, when I had a telephone call from Tony Richardson, asking me to play the part of the sluttish mother in a film of the successful stage play, *A Taste of Honey*. I hadn't ever seen the Shelagh Delaney play, and had no idea at that time who

113

Tony Richardson was, but he sounded extremely cultured and sophisticated. In the course of our conversation he told me that he came from Oldham too. His father was a chemist there. Well, that was all very nice, but I did wish I was better informed about my proposed role in the film, and about the Woodfall Films company who were planning to make it. When my agent entered into negotiations on my behalf, he was not exactly encouraged by the fact that Mr Richardson intended to make the whole thing on location. It all sounded very precarious, and when I was offered either a percentage of the profits or £1,500, my agent said it would be much better for me to take the cash because there might not be any profits. Alas, I was badly advised. The film was a huge success, and if only I had taken a share of the profits instead, as Albert Finney did for the same company's next major production, *Tom Jones*, I too would probably have had a Rolls Royce.

A Taste of Honey heralded a series of happy events and the most important of these was that I found myself pregnant again. This time everything seemed to be going according to plan. A great deal of the credit must go to Daniel and Georgina, because once I had relaxed and stopped worrying so much about having a baby of my own, since I already had them to love, nature was able to take control. I went to a gynaecologist early in my pregnancy, and was kept under strict supervision, being told to take things easily. I did no outside work at all, and prayed I would carry my baby to the full term. As an extra precaution, a stitch was put into my womb during the second month. So I settled into a temporary state of domesticity. With Sheila, our nanny, and Ivor, our housekeeper, I sometimes felt a bit superfluous hanging about the house, as they took charge of things beautifully, but I liked to think the place looked nicer when I was at home all the time, with pleasantly

114

arranged flowers, and a more balanced variety of food on the table, and the children received all my attention.

Brighton was proving to be a good place to live, especially at a time when I was having an enforced rest. We were able to see friends regularly, and I loved having the opportunity to see those theatre friends who came to Brighton on tour. I would give them high tea after they had done a matinée, and then see them off to their evening performance. I didn't feel the least bit envious. I was only too happy to wash up after they had gone, and help Sheila to put the children to bed.

A lovely early spring day dawned on 2 February 1962. The sun was shining and the sea was calm. In the morning Bill and I decided to take the children down to our beach hut for a picnic. While we were enjoying ourselves I gradually became aware that those vague pains, with which I had now become so familiar, were becoming persistent. This time I just knew that everything was going to be all right. This was not a premature baby as the others had been. I thought it was wise to leave, so we locked up the beach hut and went home, where we telephoned the nursing home to say I was on my way. Of course I was nervous, but as we drove along I was also very happy. How different it was this time; just Bill and me, with two healthy children already at home. No ambulances with emergency bells ringing, as there had been before. My nervousness was stilled once we reached the nursing home. All the nurses seemed to be smiling and full of confidence, and I was given a light and comfortable room on the ground floor.

The stitch in my womb had been removed ten days previously, and I was told I was to have a normal delivery. Bill stayed, and we watched television until eight o'clock, when he was sent home because the experts said nothing would happen until the next morning. Oh, how I wished he had stayed, because things did start to happen, and instructions had been given that no pain-killers were to be administered during the first stage. My courage deserted me, and I was very frightened. It was the longest night I have ever experienced. The only nurse on duty was busy with other babies and patients. Eventually the doctor, Mrs Beynon, arrived, and I was taken to the delivery room. When I was grabbing wildly at the gas and air machine, and hanging on to anyone within reach, baby William arrived. There were some strange faces around me, as specialists had been called in 'just in case'. With my previous history they were taking no chances. But all the extra precautions proved unnecessary. William weighed only 5½ pounds, but he was perfectly healthy, and so was I. We looked upon him as our third child rather than our first, and he was a tremendous joy to us.

I was able to feed William myself for three months, but it led to a few complications. When he was six weeks old I had to do a TV commercial, and rather than let him miss a feed I took him to the studio with me. There were certain times when everything had to stop for William, if he happened to be hungry. After a few minutes of my absence, the assistant director would be hovering outside the dressing room door, one eye on his watch, asking plaintively, 'Hasn't he finished yet?'

A few weeks later somebody telephoned to ask if I would have some family background photographs taken for publicity for the new musical. I agreed, and was told the photographers would come the following morning. I was upstairs in the nursery next morning when Bill came in and said the photographers had arrived. I walked downstairs into the large dining-room-cum-playroom, carrying William. I thought there was rather a lot of equipment just for a few photographs, but I sat down on the sofa, facing what looked suspiciously like a television camera. Then a familiar voice said from behind me, 'Hello, Dora,' and the owner of the familiar voice walked in. It was Eamonn Andrews. 'Hello, Eamonn,' I said shakily. 'What are you doing here?' It didn't take long to explain, and his next words were, 'Dora Bryan — This is your life!'

The cameras began to roll as they filmed the intro-duction to what would take place in the evening at the studios. I was so taken aback that I said exactly what I felt — 'Oh, how marvellous!' And so it was, but this was *not* what the doctor ordered. A nursing mother needs peace and quiet. It was the start of a long exciting day for me, and marked the occasion of William's introduction to the bottle.

I rushed around and found myself something to wear, and in the afternoon kissed the children good-bye, told the nanny they could sit up and watch the programme, and caught a train to London, and the BBC television studios. Sometimes *This is Your Life* can be rather sad, or even occasionally embarrassing, and for some of the 'subjects' it is clearly something of an ordeal. This one was great fun, and just like a party. I enjoyed every minute of it. One after another, in came so many of my favourite people. There was dear Auntie Jeff, my landlady when I had been at Colchester Rep; Joan Heal, with whom I'd always had such fun in revues; lovely Gladys Henson, who played the role of my mother in the film *The Cure for Love*, and young Robert Henrey, whom I had last seen as a small boy when we made the film *The Fallen Idol*, and who now was a handsome young man about town. They even brought on stage the ticket collector from the train, who on the night before my wedding had made me take my dog along to the luggage van, because he wasn't allowed in my sleeper. How on earth did they find him, I wondered. I was hoping that the BBC would have

117

filmed a message from my brother John in South Africa. It never occurred to me that they would have gone to all the trouble and expense of flying him from Cape Town, and I must admit that when he walked on to the stage with his wife Marguerite, I cried a little from sheer happiness.

The producer had pulled a fast one by having Daniel rushed up to London by car with the nanny, and when he was brought on stage I was so surprised that I turned on my poor husband in front of the cameras and said, 'What on earth is Daniel doing out at this time of night?' That raised the biggest laugh of the evening.

After a lovely party, my brother John and his wife came back home with us and stayed on for a while. They were able to be present a few days later at the British Academy Film Awards dinner, to which I had been invited, having been nominated for an award for my part in *A Taste of Honey*. I was happy just to be nominated, and to share the evening with Bill, John and Marguerite, who were so proud of me. Deborah Kerr was nominated for *The Sundowners*, and Hayley Mills for *Whistle Down the Wind*. In view of that sort of competition I simply couldn't believe it when my name was read out as the best actress of 1961. Rita Tushingham, who played my daughter in the film, received the award for the most promising newcomer, and there was yet another award made to *A Taste of Honey* for the best script, which was by Shelagh Delaney and Tony Richardson. So this film, about which there had been so many doubts at the outset, was a huge success. Peter Finch received the Best Actor award that year for *No Love for Johnnie*, and Sophia Loren was given the award for the best performance by a foreign actress for *Two Women*.

Rita Tushingham and I were invited to the Cannes Film Festival, which proved to be a great experience,

118

and very amusing. I didn't consider myself particularly sophisticated at that time, nor was Rita, who was much younger than I. Cannes at the time of the Film Festival was a whole new world. We had to mix with people on the selling and business side of films, and were invited to parties, and to dinners at all the best restaurants with producers and their wives. The wives seemed extremely glamorous, attired in their minks and gorgeous dresses and jewellery. My one major luxury was my mink stole, which I thought added a touch of class, and Rita had a pretty woolly one, which she wore with great style. I'm afraid neither of us provided much competition for the producers' wives, nor were we a match for the glamour girls on the beach as we disported ourselves in our bikinis. At one very smart dinner there was a selection of crudités on the table. I knew what to do with them as I'd encountered them before. Rita did not wait to find out the form, but promptly complained to the waiter that the vegetables weren't cooked, and asked if she could please have some cooked ones. Then she asked for Coke to drink instead of wine, which seemed a perfectly reasonable request to me, but the waiters were very snooty about it. Everyone could see that we were green about the high life of the film world, but we thoroughly enjoyed ourselves, and to the delight of the press, played up this angle of being down-to-earth, no-nonsense girls from Lancashire. Rita hailed from Liverpool, and must have been about nineteen at the time. So the pressmen began to ask us what we thought of Cannes, and French food, and we gave them the answers they wanted. We may have been new to the scene in the South of France, and the ballyhoo of a film festival, but we certainly weren't as naive and daft as we pretended to be. We gave the reporters some good copy by bemoaning the lack of fish and chips, and when I was asked my opinion of a

119

beautiful gourmet version of onion pie, I delivered the deflating verdict: 'They cook onions here the way we in Lancashire use them to cure colds!' The newspapers loved it.

Bill came out and joined me at The Carlton Hotel in Cannes for one night, then we drove off after the festival ended to have a few days by ourselves, while Rita and the rest of our group flew back to London. William was only a few months old, and I did not want to spend too long away from home, but it was a very glamorous, happy time, which was followed by a trip to Helsinki, of all places, to collect an award there on the borders of Russia. This time I didn't have Rita with me, so there was no laughing and joking. It was all deadly serious, as were the people. Their award ceremony, which to them was full of glamour and luxury, seemed dreary when compared with the no-expense-spared atmosphere of Cannes.

Inevitably something had to go wrong after all this success and happiness, and that 'something' came in the form of *Gentlemen Prefer Blondes*, the show in which I played Lorelei Lee and sang the number 'Diamonds Are a Girl's Best Friend'. The public loved it, but the critics were really vicious. We had such a wonderful opening night. There were cheers for my performance, and the kind *Daily Mirror* said the reception 'was like a Hampden roar'. Most other papers were not so kind, and within a few months of being applauded by the critics for *A Taste of Honey*, I was torn apart for my performance in *Gentlemen Prefer Blondes*. I suppose I must have been a little disappointing after Marilyn Monroe's version, but the bad reviews shattered me. My first reaction was, 'This has ruined my career. Thank goodness I have three lovely children who can't read.' Anita Loos, who created Lorelei Lee, said in public that she thought I fitted the character better than anyone else she had seen. That was at least encouraging, but after those awful reviews we needed more than that. If we were to keep the show running we were going to have to fight back and prove the critics wrong. I went on stage the second night shaking with nerves, convinced that the audience had read all the worst notices, and were wishing they had never bought tickets. But I was determined to show 'em. That was the way we all felt, and because of that determination *Blondes* lasted for nine months, despite the critics.

During the run of the show I became pregnant again. I started to sort out maternity clothes once more, and some of William's baby things. But it was not to be. At Christmas in 1962 I endured for the third time the sad experience of losing a child. This time there was no time to mope. After a few days I was back in the show, and when it finished I went into rehearsals of *Six of One* at the Adelphi Theatre. Life was too happily full to leave time for dreaming of what might have been. And yet . . . sometimes I would arrive home late at night and look at the children in the nursery, or notice my maternity clothes in the wardrobe, or maybe even see a new baby in a pram in the street, and I would think wistfully, 'Oh, it would be nice to have just one more.' But it would have turned poor Bill prematurely grey. Mind you, I've always thought a man looks very distinguished with grey hair . . .

Alan Melville, who wrote so many wonderful revue sketches for me, was always amazed at how Bill and I coped with such a household. He wrote one monologue loosely based on scenes he had witnessed in my home, which I did at the Adelphi. It depicted me, speaking in my best actressy voice, answering the phone to a well-known producer, and trying to keep the children quiet at the same time. Supposedly Daniel (aged three), was drinking someone's gin and tonic with obvious

121

enjoyment, Georgina (a year younger) was eating dog biscuits, and William (just a baby) was ensconced contentedly in the coal bucket, while the dog was making a meal of my latest television script. Bill was sitting in the middle of it all, watching *Match of the Day*. The monologue and telephone conversation were almost true to life.

Yet looking back, it was the time I was at my happiest. Life was very full and busy.

Most parents want more for their children than they had themselves. I wanted mine to have exactly what I had: a happy, secure childhood. Not that they noticed when I exhausted myself by rushing home after rehearsals or performances. They were nearly always out playing, or visiting their friends. Many times when they have been ill, I have caught the evening train from Brighton to do a show in London and have thought, 'What am I doing all this for? My place is at home.' I'm sure all actresses go through this. Travelling up to London on the train on a cold winter evening, leaving the family at teatime, and seeing from the train window other people's houses lit up, and families sitting around their tables, I've thought, 'I'll give it all up.' But once in the theatre those feelings have to be forgotten.

In 1963 I was as busy as ever after *Gentlemen Prefer Blondes*. Producer Peter Bridge and I got together and devised a show which became *Six of One*, the title meaning six forms of entertainment in which I had worked — concert party, pantomime, situation comedy, revue, musical comedy and variety. We opened in Manchester, and the opening night was a shambles. Peter came round to see me. The director had fled! I said, 'Send for Billy Chappell.' Billy had guided and directed me in all those revues that had been so successful, and I trusted him implicitly. Billy arrived, and warned me it would be hard work. He whipped us

122

9. At a Variety Club lunch with *(standing, left to right)* Vera Lynn, Jack Warner. Anna Neagle, Margaret Johnston, Bob Monkhouse, and *(sitting, left to right)* Pat Burke, Maurice Chevalier, Ingrid Bergman and me.

10. With Murray Melvin and Rita Tushingham in *A Taste of Honey*.

11. With Tamsin Olivier, my god-daughter, and her dad, 1963.

12. "All I want for Christmas is a Beatle."

13. With John Blythe in *Hello, Dolly!*

14. Hopefully off for a walk. Our mother's help, Susan,
William, Daniel, me, Bill and Georgina.

15. With Cliff Richard in *Two a Penny*.

16. The family on the way to South Africa.

into shape unmercifully, with all-day rehearsals and evening performances, new material going in, and old material coming out. I have never learnt so many sketches and songs in such a short time. In fact, Peter took us out to dinner one night after the show, and when the menu was put in front of me I started to learn it.

It was worth all the hard work. We opened at the Adelphi Theatre in London and were a big success. We had a very talented cast — Sheila O'Neill, Amanda Barrie, David Toguri, Denis Lotis, John Hewer and Richard Wattis. A very happy show to be in. During the run I was asked to record a Christmas song. It was given to me on the night after the show, and I rewrote some of it. We recorded it next day, and off it went into the charts the first week. It was 'All I Want for Christmas is a Beatle', and was played on radio constantly. I had to appear on *Top of the Pops*, and it was voted 'the best bad record of 1963'. I was quite pleased with my place in the charts. I met the Beatles a few times through this record, and at that stage in their careers I found them very bright, unspoilt, and friendly boys. I don't think any Christmas goes by without the record being played on the radio.

After a successful run, we took the whole family to South Africa where I was to do a revue in Cape Town and Johannesburg. This was a wonderful opportunity to see my brother John, Marguerite and my three nieces, as they lived in Cape Town. It also enabled us to have a lovely two-week sea journey. I was returning to do *The Dora Bryan Show* at the Opera House, Manchester for a ten-week Christmas run. A clever young magician, Dennis Spicer, was going to be starring in the show with me, but as we were returning home on board ship we were informed that he had been tragically killed in a car crash. Our sea trip had to be curtailed, so we left the ship at Madeira and flew home, as I had to start rehearsing the show with the Kaye Sisters who were replacing Dennis. That sounds odd, I know. It reminds me of the time when I was ill during the run of a summer show, and I gather that the management, making an announcement before the show, said that owing to the indisposition of Miss Dora Bryan, her part would be played by Rawicz and Landauer.

While my career was careering on, Bill retired from his cricket and bought a small guest house in Brighton, the Glencoe, which did very well, but we decided to turn it into flats and install Bill's Mum and Dad in one, and my beloved sister-in-law Adah and her husband in another, and let the rest. We then bought a bigger hotel, Northumberland Hall, and moved ourselves to a large house on the sea front, next to the Glencoe that was, and our relatives. Northumberland Hall Hotel had a neon sign, which blew down in one of the severe south coast gales. Now 'NORTHUMBERLAND HALL HOTEL' in terms of neon lighting, was a very big sign, and it was much cheaper to replace it with a short sign, so it became BRYAN'S HOTEL, which ran quite smoothly.

But life never stands still and Bill had another idea. He had had his eye on Clarges Hotel ever since I was pregnant with William, and we spotted it while walking along the sea front, the only exercise I was permitted at that time, apart from swimming. Eventually Clarges came on the market, so we bought it and sold Bryan's Hotel. Clarges, with its sixty bedrooms, was Bill's biggest undertaking. We all ate in there quite a lot, as it saved the cooking and washing up! If we were eating in our own home, I would go into Clarges with my shopping basket, just like Red Riding Hood, and say to the chef, 'Could I have some steak and some prawns, love?' It was lovely, and just like having my own private Harrods next door.

We were constantly trying to pick up useful ideas from other hotels we stayed at, and always looked at them through professional eyes. Sometimes I would walk into a hotel room and find Bill investigating all the fittings and furniture to see how they were made. He would take menus and slip them into his pocket so that he could cost everything, and in a Birmingham hotel I once found him lying under the bed, looking to see how the bedside tables were attached to the wall.

Nothing every runs entirely smoothly, and there were still the odd staff problems from time to time, some more odd than others. There was the occasion when the chef tripped over in the kitchen while he was cooking dinner. He had a glass in his hand at the time, and as he fell the glass broke. His head had a very deep cut, which was bleeding profusely. It was padded up with a napkin, and Bill sent him along to the hospital, detailing Alfie, the kitchen porter, to go along with him. They made a strange couple, as Steve the chef was 6 feet tall, and Alfie was only 4 feet 11 inches in his socks. It was quite amusing to think of little Alfie looking after Steve, and it was a case of the blind leading the blind, but at least Alfie did his best. They piled into a taxi, and as the whole thing had been organized so quickly, Alfie didn't really know why they were going to the hospital. 'What's the matter, Steve?' he asked, as they drove off. In reply, Steve took the blood-stained napkin away from his head and Alfie promptly fainted. When they reached the hospital, a trolley was brought for Alfie, and Steve had to wait for attention. Having been stitched up, Steve went in search of Alfie, and found him in bed having tests done. He had been wheeled off on his trolley through the Casualty Department, and had kept seeing accident cases and bottles of blood, at the sight of which he passed out again. The result was that Steve came back and carried on cooking the dinner, and Alfie was kept in for two days for observation.

Life was a constant battle between such domestic dramas as this, and comedy and drama in the theatre. It was never dull, and anyway I loved the challenge of doing several things at once. We did a production of Shaw's *Too True to be Good* in Manchester in 1965, as part of a tour before taking it to the Edinburgh Festival. It was at the Manchester Opera House, and at the same time I was booked for a week's cabaret at Mr Smith's Club — also in Manchester. That was fine, because after the evening performance of the play I would go and do my late night cabaret. All was well until the club manager read in the paper that I was in the cast of the Shaw play as well. This sort of schizophrenic deploying of one's talent is known in the theatre as 'doing a double', and the club manager said to me, 'I hear you're doing a double this week.'

'Well, yes, I suppose you could say that,' I replied. 'I'm at the Opera House, but I'm doing a straight play there.'

'Sorry,' he said, 'but as far as I'm concerned you're doing a double, and you'll have to take less money.'

I didn't see why I should. After all, I was doing two lots of work. But the club manager was adamant that as I wasn't appearing exclusively for him that week my money would have to be reduced, which it was. It all seemed a great fuss about nothing. The Opera House hadn't complained.

At the mid-week matinée of *Too True to be Good* the Manchester audience was small, and producer Frank Dunlop came round to see me in the interval to tell me of the conversation he had overheard between two elderly ladies who had obviously seen me before, but they must have been used to seeing me in musicals.

126

Because there weren't many people in the house their voices were quite audible. I was playing Nurse Sweetie, and had been on stage some time when one lady said to her friend, 'Do you think that's her? The one dressed as a nurse?'

'No,' replied her companion. 'That's not her. She usually sings when she comes on.'

I wonder what they made of Shaw? They must have been very disappointed that there were no songs. After the Edinburgh Festival the play went to London, opening at the Strand Theatre, and then transferring to the Garrick. It was a good cast, with George Cole, Alastair Sim, Athene Seyler, June Ritchie and James Bolam, and it settled down for a long run, but I left the cast to do *The Dora Bryan Show* at the Royal Court in Liverpool, with David Nixon and a very funny Liverpool comic, Johnny Hackett. It was great fun, and during the run of the show we all stayed with my sister-in-law in Oldham, so it was a nice 'family time'.

While I was doing this, there came an offer of a part in *The King's Mare* by Anita Loos. I was to play opposite Keith Michell, and the part was Anne of Cleves. Because one is always looking forward to the next adventure, I agreed. There wasn't going to be much time between the end of my show in Liverpool and the opening of *The King's Mare*, so I spent a lot of hours between performances learning the very long and complicated part. There were long speeches about heraldry, I remember.

Things never happen singly; it's either all or nothing and I was surprised to receive a call from my agent to say that Binkie Beaumont had been in touch with him, and could I join Binkie, David Merrick and himself for lunch at Scott's, which was a very smart restaurant in Piccadilly, sadly no longer there. By then I had learnt all the part for *The King's Mare*, only to be told at lunch that

I would not be doing it after all, but instead would be taking over from Mary Martin in *Hello, Dolly!* at Drury Lane. How they got me out of the other show I never found out. Of course I was a bit annoyed to think of all the hours I had spent learning a script for nothing, but this was completely overshadowed by the excitement of the opportunity I was about to have. What a thrill to be playing the lead at Drury Lane, and to be taking over from a great star like Mary Martin. What glamour those American musical stars had! Recently I have been working with Cyd Charisse, who was with MGM for so many years. Her husband, Tony Martin, was always around, and I was forever asking them about all the old stars. They were only too happy to talk about those wonderful days of the Hollywood musical, and I still think that Judy Garland was the most talented of all. Larry Grayson and I are both besotted about her, and I will watch anything she was in. My garden contains Judy Garland roses, I'm an honorary member of her fan club, and I read every word I can about her. I just wish I could have known her better.

Way back in 1960 I was working in Bournemouth doing a summer season with Al Read and Marty Wilde, when Brian Blades, a friend of mine, telephoned to tell me that he had two tickets for a Judy Garland Sunday concert at the London Palladium, and asked if I would like to go. I told Bill that he would have to look after Daniel, and I was off on the London train. Oh, the excitement! I knew George, the stage door keeper at the Palladium, and after the performance I asked him if we could go in to see her. We went into the star dressing room, where Judy was sitting all alone in a dreary dressing gown, without the caps on her teeth — so ordinary, and yet to me so wonderful. We told her how marvellous she was, and what fans we were, and I explained to her that I was 'on the stage' too. She was just so like one of us that I couldn't believe it. She offered us a glass of wine, but when she produced the bottle of Liebfraumilch she realized she didn't have a corkscrew. Instead, she invited us to go to the Mayfair Hotel where she was staying, and said we could have some wine with her there later. We couldn't believe it.

When we arrived at the Mayfair she was charming, and showed us photographs of her children. Dirk Bogarde was at her feet, as he had been on stage at the London Palladium, where she had sung one of her songs to him. Her husband Sid Luft was very attentive to her, and Shirley Bassey was singing her heart out in a corner with a small group of musicians. What an evening it was! I stayed till the last possible moment, reluctant to leave, and caught the milk train back to Bournemouth.

I had to get myself into good shape for *Hello Dolly*, and as there was a month to spare before we started rehearsals I went to a travel agent and said, 'I have a month's holiday. Where can we go for a really nice holiday in the sun?'

'Las Palmas,' said the travel agent.

We left it to him to book everything; a three-day boat trip to Las Palmas, two weeks there, and a three-day boat trip home. Lovely! But he must have thought it was a no-expense-spared holiday. We had three de luxe cabins on the ship, and found he had booked a three-bedroomed suite at the hotel in Las Palmas. This was no package holiday. We arrived to find champagne, flowers and chocolates in the suite. Bill and I looked at each other. I looked behind the door and saw the prices of the rooms listed. Horrified, I ran down to Reception and said we only required two bedrooms and no sitting room, as our nanny preferred to sleep with the children, and we felt it was cosier without the sitting room.

It would have been unthinkable to have had all our meals in the dining-room, as there were six of us, and I'd had a peep at the menu. So I found the equivalent of a corner shop in Las Palmas, with sliced bread, cheese, ham, fruit, milk and cereals. Room service was very good indeed. Soup for one came on a trolley in an enormous tureen, and was ample for six. We had lovely picnics in our rooms, taking crockery and cutlery from the trolleys to use for our feasts. I kept the cutlery in the underwear drawer and the crockery in the wardrobe. The English pub did very good sausage and chips, and egg and chips, followed by ice cream, so that took care of the evening meal. I was alone in the bedroom one day, preparing one of our indoor picnics, and needed some extra spoons for the 'soup for one' I had ordered. I had seen the used trays along the corridor and set off in my bra and pants. As I was collecting the spoons I heard the bedroom door slam in the wind. I was locked out. I lurked in that corridor for ages before the family arrived. At the same time, the floor waiter arrived with the trolley and tureen and 'soup for one'. I felt very uncomfortable with spoons in my bra and pants.

For some reason the children never questioned why we ate in the bedroom, except Daniel, who wasn't too keen on being fobbed off with sandwiches. He wanted a sit-down lunch one day in the hotel. I replied vaguely that the hotel didn't have a dining-room. That kept him quiet until the last day, when we were all sitting around the crowded swimming pool, and he announced in a loud voice, 'Mummy, they do have a dining-room at this hotel, I've found it.' That was just one occasion when my children made me wish for a large hole to open in the ground so that I could jump into it. We treated them to dinner in the dining-room that night. They deserved it.

I was also perfectly capable of dropping my own

resounding 'clangers', and few were worse than the day I was invited on to an afternoon chat show for TyneTees Television when I was appearing in the north-east. It was a charming studio set, with the usual chairs in strategic interviewing positions, and surrounded by a series of plants, in which the protea plant featured largely. It's always nice to have something original to say on chat shows, and I did know something about these particular plants, so I thought that would make a good gambit. The programme opened, and as I hadn't been briefed about the other guest, a very pleasant lady, who was sitting next to me, I thought I'd warm up proceedings. Chat shows can be sticky sometimes, especially if the interviewees are nervous, and slight nervousness always makes me chat more. 'You really ought to get these protea plants out of here,' I said. 'They look nice, but they're terrible things really, you know.' The interviewer raised her eyebrows and politely and smilingly asked why.

'Ooh, well, they harbour beetles,' I announced sagely. 'I was once on board ship, coming back from South Africa. I'd been doing a revue out there, and the family was with me. When we sailed I was horrified to find a black beetle in my bed. The steward said it was from my farewell present of protea flowers. When the captain found out there were protea plants on board he ordered that they should all be thrown over the side.' I got into my stride, and rambled on about people feeling itchy, and the dreadful consequences of protea plants. Everyone continued to smile pleasantly, but there was a slight stiffening of the spine from the other interviewee, and I thought I detected a swift exchange of glances on set. It was not until the programme was over, and I was back in the hospitality room that it was explained to me that the protea plants decorating the studio that afternoon had all been provided by the

131

other guest on the programme, who happened to be a representative of a horticultural firm. They were hoping to import the plants. I really was upset, and hoped I didn't damage their trade too much that afternoon. How I wished that someone had told me who the other guest was before the cameras started to roll.

It was in 1966 that I went to Buckingham Palace for my lunch with the Queen and Prince Philip. I couldn't believe it when the invitation arrived. The children were so used to going everywhere with me that when I excitedly told them I had been invited to lunch at Buckingham Palace, Georgina said instantly, 'Oh, I'll wear my bridesmaid's dress!' I had to disappoint her and say that this time the invitation was just for me, but I promised to tell her all about it when I came back. Knowing we always return hospitality, Georgina automatically assumed that the Royals would be invited to visit us in return, so she said, 'When the Queen comes here, can Mrs Watkins and Fiona come?' They were her headmistress and her best friend, and quite the most important people in her life at the time. I said, 'Of course they can,' and she seemed quite happy about that.

I was rather nervous about the visit to the Palace, and pondered for ages about what to wear, finally settling for a smart little brown dress and small mink hat. It did not make things any easier when I discovered that I was the only female present — apart from the Queen, of course. No one showed me the ladies' room, and I left my coat and hat in a very ordinary room, considering it was Buckingham Palace. It contained several children's bicycles and had no mirror, so I just had to hope that my lipstick wasn't smudged and that my slip wasn't showing when we were ushered into an ante-room for sherry. There I was standing around with five men I didn't know. It was quite daunting. Then in came four corgis, who broke the tension, followed by the Queen and Prince Philip. They did their best to make us feel at home, but how can anyone be completely relaxed on such an occasion? I knelt down to greet a corgi when he trotted into the room, so at least I didn't have far to go in order to curtsey to the Queen. I was on the floor when she came in.

It was all wonderful, of course, but I just wished everyone would go away so that I could have a quiet look around the Palace. There were so many beautiful things to see, and anyway, I wanted to find a loo. Somehow I didn't relax at all. I sat next to Prince Philip at lunch. It was a very good lunch, what I can remember of it, but when the fresh fruit came round I declined. Then a large gold plate of grapes came round, complete with a neat pair of gold scissors to serve them with. I thought I could risk some grapes, so I cut myself what I thought was a dainty clump. There were far more attached to the stalk than I had anticipated, and my judgement hadn't been very good. When they were reposing on my plate I was horrified to see that they looked as though they weighed at least a pound. But one has to rise to such occasions with dignity, so I discreetly and daintily chomped my way through them as though it was quite a normal everyday occurrence for me to eat a pound of grapes at one sitting. The pips were a bit of a problem. To have filled my plate with pips would simply have drawn attention to the number of grapes I'd eaten, and as you can't drop them on the carpet under the table at Buckingham Palace, or blow them across the room, there was only one alternative. I swallowed them all.

The time came for me to take over the lead in *Hello, Dolly!*, and it was a wonderful experience. We settled into the run, and while doing 'Dolly' I was asked to play the part of Cliff Richard's mum in a film being made for the Billy Graham Organization (Billy Graham the evangelist). The film was to be called *Two a Penny*, and we were to receive £50 a week. This seemed rather a small amount to work for, but the idea intrigued me. I knew Cliff, having appeared with him in a charity show, *Night of a Hundred Stars*, when he was just eighteen. We did a number together in which he played Freddie Bartholomew and I played Shirley Temple. We sang 'Friendship', which was quite appropriate as it turned out, because we are now good friends. The Billy Graham film, on looking back, was a way of leading me into the strong faith I now have. I was extremely sceptical about Billy Graham and all his devotees. Most of us working on the film were anything but dedicated Christians, and the director, James Collier, gave no indication at the time of his own deep faith, nor did the cameraman, but there was a happy relaxed atmosphere on the film, and Cliff was always a joy to work with. When we finished filming I found myself drifting into the Bible bookshops in Brighton, and buying a few books on the Christian faith. It never occurred to me to read the Bible itself, of course. That old book on the shelf, and Mr Gideon's hotel standby, had never been delved into by me. As far as I was concerned religion was something one took for granted without doing anything too definite about it.

After the two-year run of *Hello, Dolly!* at Drury Lane we took it on tour, and when I was in Liverpool staying with the children in a rented house in Gateacre, Cliff phoned me and asked if I would see a friend of his Max Wigley. A friend of Cliff's would be a friend of mine, so of course I said I would meet him. Bill had taken the children ice skating. I was at home and full of flu when what looked like a burly footballer arrived at the back door. 'Hello, I'm Max,' he said. 'Cliff said you'd like to see me.' We sat and talked about everything under the sun, and I had no idea at first that he was the curate at the local church. Max and his wife Caroline gradually became good friends of mine.

The children had to go back to Brighton to school, and I moved into the Adelphi Hotel in Liverpool. After some long conversations with Max, he brought me an easy-to-read Bible (now very tattered and well marked). He sometimes came to have tea with me between shows, and one day he said, 'Dora, I'm sure you would like to know Jesus personally, wouldn't you? Shall we pray about it?' So with Max and Caroline I knelt in a hotel bedroom and asked Jesus into my life to share it with me, saying I wished to commit my life to Him. I didn't feel very different afterwards; there were no visions or revelations, but I did somehow feel better, as though I had taken a big step. Previously, God, in a kind of way, had been my mother. She was with God, and was a link. I reached Him through her. I was really praying to my mother when I said inwardly, 'Mum, would you speak to God, please?' She had been dead for seven years, but I knew she hadn't gone away. She was still with me. Now that it had been explained to me about the Resurrection I knew Jesus was alive too. Everything began to make sense. I am not totally committed in the way that some people are, who do their Bible study every day. I simply don't have the time, but I'm sure the Lord understands all about our different lifestyles. I am, however, a great and absolute believer in prayer, and the fact that we are led to certain places and experiences by God. We are put in positions where we can do most good — if only we care to look around.

When I'm working I don't have as much time to spend with my committed Christian friends, but I enjoy church on Sunday, and hearing all their news. Sundays are very special. Eight performances a week,

135

plus the occasional promotion for the show on radio or television makes it very hard to retain spare time or have any kind of social life. It has been suggested that theatres should open on Sundays, with the option of having Mondays off instead. I have no objection at all if other actors wish to do this, and I know a lot of people who would love to see a Sunday show. Although in principle it sounds like a good idea, it just wouldn't be the same, and certainly I would not wish to do it. This has nothing at all to do with religious grounds. I simply like my Sundays at home.

It is now twenty years since I made my commitment, and that's a long time of slithering and sliding, but I look back and see the progress I have made. If, as St Peter says, a thousand years is nothing, then I'll make it. Some time ago I started a Sunday School in my own home, because at the time our church did not have one. We were all children together, as I knew so little, but with the help of books on children's worship, we got by and had a good time. I learnt as much from the children as they learnt from me. Their prayers were very enlightening. One little girl, Sheila, requested us quite matter-of-factly not to pray any more for her grandad to get well, as he had just died, and could we now pray for a new dress for her mum, as she had nothing to wear for the funeral, and was very upset.

I once asked the children how they would feel if, when they were on the beach fishing, a complete stranger came up to them and asked them to leave their nets and fishing rods, and go with him to fish for men. One little boy said he didn't go on the beach because of the pebbles. Another said he didn't like fishing. But on the whole I think I put across the Christian message. Some of my pupils would never have gone into a church but being in my house with the bonus of orange squash and biscuits did help to keep their interest. It was sad that it all had to break up, because I had to go to Scotland for two months with a show. Diana, my mother's help, tried to carry on with it, but as she was so much younger than I was she hadn't the same authority, and according to my husband it became a rather badly run session, and very noisy. Now we have a successful Sunday School in our church, but I still remember mine with pleasure.

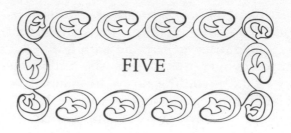

FIVE

IT WOULD BE AN EXAGGERATION TO SAY THAT MY CHILDREN grew up in a theatre dressing room, but when I was in a show they certainly spent a lot of time backstage, especially during their school holidays. When Daniel was fourteen, he was helping with props during his Christmas holiday.

I never thought William took much notice of my performance in *Hello, Dolly!*, as he was only about three years old at the time. I was proved wrong. When we took all the children to see Barbra Streisand in the film version, William, who had seen his mum in the role so many times from the side of the stage, couldn't put up with Streisand any longer. Much to my embarrassment he stood up in the cinema and shouted, 'Copy cat!'

My dressing room was always packed with children, two dogs, Lego sets and dolls, a nanny, and Bill, who had one eye on them and the other on the TV set in the corner. There wasn't much room for the sequins and feathers, and how I kept a dresser I shall never know. I did two pantomimes with Norman Vaughn, and his dressing room always seemed a haven of peace. His dressing table was so clean and tidy, while mine was just a heap of children's bits and pieces. During the run of *Hello, Dolly!* the children often came to Saturday matinées, and because the Royal Box was easily accessible, that is where they were usually installed to watch the show — if the box wasn't sold, of course. They were always accompanied by their nanny, but one afternoon she must have disappeared to go to the loo, or buy ice cream, and they were left alone in the box. I was in the middle of one of my songs and happened to look up in their direction. What met my gaze was the hair-raising sight of Daniel, leaning out of the box and busily trying to unscrew the royal coat of arms, which was a bit off-putting to say the least. I hope it didn't distract the matinée audience as much as it preoccupied me. It was very difficult to concentrate after that little episode. Then there was the business of sneezing powder being thrown down into the audience from time to time. All that sort of thing went on until it was severely stamped upon.

During summer seasons, which coincided with the long school holidays, I tried to keep the family together, and we rented places for the season, which meant that at least everyone could have a seaside holiday. I did a summer season at Blackpool with Les Dawson, Lennie Bennett and Ronnie Hilton, and we rented a lovely house with a lake at Poulton-le-Fylde. There was myself, Bill, three children, Diana, who was our mother's help, Freddy the dog, and Sooty the cat. On the inventory when we took over, just after the list of cutlery it said: 'Twelve ducks'. Those ducks must have taken one look at us all and decided they didn't like what they saw, because they took to the wing and promptly departed. I wondered why they were on the inventory. Perhaps the owners of the house thought we might be partial to roast duck.

We were in the house for eight weeks, and it is quite

surprising how much extra equipment can accumulate in that time. When the day came for the family to go home, they had collected three new chopper bikes, extra clothes, more toys, and there was also a series of pots and pans which I had bought to supplement those already in the house. We had arrived in a perfectly ordinary family car, but it was quite clear that they could not go home in the car with all that stuff, so a friend said he would bring a van. It arrived on the Sunday night, and was a large black 1930s ambulance. The children were thrilled. It didn't seem possible, but even that vehicle was only just big enough to take everything. Somehow we packed in all the luggage, the cat, the dog, and the bikes, plus two of the children. Daniel had to get in through the back window because it was so full. Bill rode next to Joe, the driver, and with a top speed of thirty miles an hour they sailed forth to Brighton, where I understand their arrival caused quite a stir. I was left to close up the house and move to a hotel for the last four weeks of the summer season, and, much as I love my family, I must say that it was sheer luxury. I wonder if the twelve ducks flew back to their lake?

I think without a doubt my favourite time with the children was the summer season at Great Yarmouth with *The Dora Bryan Show* on the Wellington Pier, once again with Johnny Hackett and Mark Wynter.

It was very difficult to find a house to rent for the children's eight-week summer holiday, as we were in competition with Engelbert Humperdinck and Charlie Drake, who were playing at the other theatres. Bill had made two fruitless trips to try and find somewhere for us, but then he telephoned while I was rehearsing a TV show, and said the only place he could find was 'a bit primitive', and eight miles out of Yarmouth. I went up to see it after rehearsal one day. It was certainly different, and we had no choice but to take it — a low-built house standing in two acres. The owners, Mr and Mrs Varney, a very nice couple, lived in one end. Their son was Prince Philip's bodyguard. But, oh dear, after our own home it seemed very basic, with hot water heated by a boiler in the kitchen, which became the bane of my life for eight weeks.

My nanny informed me she wouldn't be coming to Great Yarmouth as she had just become engaged, and couldn't bear the separation from her boy friend. This didn't trouble me too much as the children were old enough to manage with the help of a young local girl. I thought happily that I'd get a nice young girl in Great Yarmouth. But all the nice young girls in Great Yarmouth were working in the hotels, and were not interested in being tucked away in the depths of the country with no bus service. Bill wasn't going to be much help, as he had just bought Clarges Hotel in Brighton and wouldn't be with me all the time, so I would just have to make the best of things.

Burgh Castle was a lovely unspoilt village, and Norfolk was so different from Sussex. I loved it. The children became real little Huckleberry Finns during their stay in the country. The Varneys were always discreetly around, we felt safe and happy — and we managed. I would put the children on trust to go to bed when I drove off to do my twice-nightly show, knowing the Varneys were there in case of any strange happenings. Some nights when I drove back into the grounds of the house with my headlights full on, I would find myself dodging hedgehogs, and would see faces at the windows. But I never minded. The children were wonderful company, particularly that never-to-be-forgotten bright starry night when the first men landed on the moon. The children were soon bored with watching the event on TV, and were far more

141

interested in the moonlit garden, so we went out there and were convinced we saw the men walking about on the moon!

The alternative to leaving the children at the house was to take them with me to the theatre, and let them have all the free fairground rides and games of Bingo they wanted. They were thoroughly spoiled by the attendants, and won so many teddies, golliwogs and china figurines that I could have opened up a shop in my dressing room at the end of the pier. My dresser was amazed at our lifestyle. She told me she had been 'treated for nerves' for years, and was on eight pills a day — more if necessary, but by the end of the season with me she was cured.

On Georgina's ninth birthday we had her party on Sunday, my day off, and invited all the local children. My dresser came out to Burgh Castle for the day to help. I was feeling a bit overwrought with it all, so I asked her if she had one of her pills with her. She had, and I took it. Just one pill, and I felt like Alice in Wonderland for the rest of the day!

When the children grew up, summer seasons were much more peaceful, and I enjoyed one in Weymouth in 1983. Daniel was stage manager for the show. It was a lovely hot summer, which wasn't good news for the theatre, and never is, because all the holidaymakers stay on the beach until dark.

I had a 32-foot caravan, and decided to take it to live in during the season, because I wanted to take the two dogs with me, and they would not have been welcome at a hotel. I found a nice site at a farm in Dorset, about eighteen miles from the theatre. I received permission from Sir Joseph Wild to take the van there, as it was part of the Wild estate, and I had a lovely landlady, Eileen Butt, who became a good friend to all the family. Daniel and I kept moving the caravan around so that we could get the best possible site, and in the end I had a marvellous view over the whole of Dorset. Bill used to come at weekends, but he hated staying in the caravan, and stayed mostly in Eileen's farmhouse leaving me to the bunk beds.

One morning I got out of bed, looked out of the van, and discovered that all our garden furniture had completely disappeared. I thought it must have been stolen, but in fact the cows had trampled on everything, and it had been dragged down the field. Eileen was most upset, and asked her workmen to fence me in, so after that I was much happier, and became quite involved with local village life. We had a fête to raise money for the village church, and then word seemed to get around that I wasn't averse to rural life. Dorset is a big county, and I've never known so many village fêtes. Sometimes I would open two fêtes and then go on to do the evening show, so I rather wore myself out, driving from place to place. I loved Dorset, which is a beautiful area, and even began to look around for houses there, but I realized it was just a bit too far from London.

I have already touched upon the domestic issue of nannies, on which I'm a great expert, and while the children were small, nannies really did become a great feature of life, not to mention a hazard. The trouble with nannies (as I was reliably informed by another expert), is that they become drunk with power. They are in positions of great responsibility, and are often in charge of the entire household at times, which is apt to go to their heads. They also know that most families for whom they work have accounts at various shops, giving domestic staff easy purchasing power. In the case of our nannies it seemed to be food shops which had an attraction. One Christmas when our combined relatives came to stay with us, they were regaled for their return journeys with beautiful tins of biscuits,

143

cooked chickens, and bottles of vintage port to tide them over. Very nice, except that I wasn't the one dishing out all the goodies, and didn't know we even had them in the house. It was our nanny distributing the largesse, and only when she departed did the full contents of the kitchen cupboards come to light. Her name was Mabel, and she had gourmet tastes. We found the cupboards stuffed with marrons glacés, tinned woodcock, tins of wildly expensive biscuits, boxes of exotic chocolates, and items we would never eat. I came to an arrangement with the shopkeeper to return it all to him, which was a bit embarrassing. 'Don't worry,' he said understandingly. 'This sort of thing often happens.' I wondered why none of my friends had warned me about turning the nanny loose on a grocery account, because we were always discussing our nanny problems. Theatre families especially, who have to rely so much upon household help, are particularly prone to disasters.

Bill and I gave a little party on one occasion, and the Oliviers were due to come. Joan arrived alone and said, 'Larry will be along later. The nanny's got her arm stuck in the washing machine. The fire brigade is at home trying to release her, and Larry's fascinated. He wants to know why they aren't wearing their lovely helmets.' Larry eventually arrived, and related the whole saga with great humour, but when the poor girl came next day to have tea with our nanny, as part of the social round, her arm was heavily bandaged. The fire brigade — even without their helmets — had managed to release her, but not without some physical damage being done.

We appointed a very nice Geordie girl called Julie, who had an almost incomprehensible accent, but once we became accustomed to it we all got along very well. The trouble was that Julie was very homesick for the north-east, and asked if she could have her friend to stay with her to keep her company. She would share Julie's room and help with the work, but we need only pay one of them, she said. That sounded like a fair arrangement, so the friend duly presented herself in Brighton. She too was called Julie, and was about six feet tall. Inevitably, they became known as Big Julie and Little Julie, or collectively as the Two Julies, which sounded like a music hall act. Certainly they were a couple of great entertainers, but not quite in that sense. They entertained everyone — in our house. I know the folks in the north-east are noted for their hospitality, but this became ridiculous. The boy who delivered the evening paper was invited in for coffee; then there was the window cleaner, the various delivery men, and the many friends they made during their sorties to the local dance hall. Life was one long party for them, and the children adored them both. We were a little concerned about security, as they didn't seem to be particularly selective in their friends, so it all had to come to a stop. After they left we had a burglary, and all the Staffordshire china disappeared. We had no proof of where it went, but we did wonder whether it was anything to do with the many outsiders who had crossed our doors during the reign of the Two Julies.

Marion presented a different problem. She became totally stage-struck. I understood that perfectly, so through some local contacts I arranged for her to join one of the amateur groups in Brighton. She was thrilled to death, and threw herself into a production of *Orpheus in the Underworld*. On the night of the show, while dancing the cancan, she took a tumble, injuring her coccyx. Upon recovery, she decided she would like to become a model. She was a very attractive girl, so I invited my two friends Larry and Bill, who ran the London School of Modelling in Bond Street, to meet her. We had some other guests, and I asked Marion to come up and join us. When she made her entrance I could hardly believe my eyes, and neither could Larry and Bill. They must have thought I was completely mad. In she came, clad in black fishnet tights, a short tight black silk skirt, and a clinging gold lamé top. She was plastered with make-up, and looked for all the world like someone going to a fancy dress party as a French prostitute. 'This is my nanny,' I announced, and never had there been such a ridiculous introduction. Mouths dropped open and all eyes popped. The only follow-up I could think of in my state of shock was 'Marion, where are you going?'

The story of Marion took a very sad turn. She eventually found a job modelling and selling in a wholesale factory, and we learned that she had suffered a nervous breakdown, and had had a lobotomy operation. She was in hospital for some time, and when I visited, the psychiatrist said, 'You know, Mrs Lawton, she was never happier than when she worked with you.' We offered to have her back with us as a general help, and said we would give her a home. When we went to meet her train she wasn't on it. I phoned the hospital and told them, and they assured me they had put her on the train. Investigations proved that she had found her way back to her home town of Liverpool, and, tragically, she took her own life.

Another drama came with the nanny who wanted to be known as 'Mr Margaret'. We should have known at the outset that she really wanted to look after me! I came home after a show one night to find her door locked, and ropes tied from the handle on to the radiator on the opposite wall. Bill explained that he had found her not only drunk, but high on drugs. He had sent for the doctor, who had advised him to lock her in her room, as she shouldn't be at large in the house, and

146

could not be turned out in that condition, especially with snow on the ground. I was devastated to think that she had put my children to bed when under the influence of drink and drugs. Next morning I went in to her to find her in a very demanding mood. She announced that it was her day off, and she would like breakfast in bed. Bill appeared in a flash, unprepared to put up with any more of this nonsense. 'Out! Now!' he ordered. We gave her half an hour to pack, and she went off into the snow in a taxi, winding down the cab window to deliver her parting shot. 'Are you sure you're doing the right thing, Daddy?' she called out. Funny. She'd come to us with excellent references . . .

Fortunately, later nannies were wonderful. There was Sheila, Susan, and Irene, and as the children grew older I had mother's helps. Dear Dianne, who was just fifteen, was a real little mother. But the time had come for a change of plan. Bill's elder sister Adah was a tower of strength when we were going through nanny dramas. The constant procession of unsuitable candidates made me feel very insecure, and I would be on the telephone to Adah to say, 'Can you come and stay for a week? I've got to get rid of this nanny.' And dear Adah would leave her husband behind, and come and sort me out. Bill's parents were already living in Brighton, and we persuaded Adah and her husband to come and live there too. I have always been a great one for 'family', and it's good, especially in the case of adopted children, to have as many relatives around as possible. We became rather like Oldham-by-the-Sea by the time the clan had descended upon Brighton. After that, no matter what happened, all the nannies were ultimately responsible to Adah, who was in charge, and that took a great weight off my mind. It also gave the children a stability which they needed. I didn't have an elder sister, but as Adah was Bill's elder sister she became mine too. Although she wasn't old enough to be my mother, we had a kind of mother–daughter relationship in a way, and went through a lot together. Sadly, in recent years she has become the second member of our family to become crippled with arthritis, the other one being our son Daniel.

We first became aware that Daniel was suffering discomfort in his feet when he was twelve years old. He complained that his feet ached, but as he was otherwise perfectly healthy this wasn't taken too seriously — just 'growing pains', we were told, and another diagnosis was that he had 'paper boy's complaint', but I was never sure why paper boys should have aching feet these days — most of them ride bikes. It sounded like a version of 'housemaid's knee', which is now often given quite a different name because there aren't many housemaids who spend hours on their knees. The doctor said Daniel should give up games at school while the condition persisted. As he grew into his teens he developed other symptoms, but it is always difficult with a sensitive child to know when there is something really wrong and when it is partly imagination. One wants to be sympathetic, yet also wants to discourage 'making a fuss', so we went along with the chest pains and the back pains, having them checked, and feeling reassured that there was nothing seriously wrong. He was on tour with a play as stage manager when he was seventeen, and I was on tour elsewhere. He telephoned me backstage one day and asked, 'Mum, do you know what spondylitis is?' I groaned inwardly, as I thought that Daniel had found himself another disease, perhaps by reading about it or hearing somebody talk about it. I didn't know about spondylitis, I told him. Why did he want to know about that?

'I had some pains and went to the theatre doctor,' replied Daniel. 'He gave me a prescription for some

148

tablets, and when I went to the chemist he said they were for spondylitis.'

By this time I was worried to death, and when Daniel came home he went straight to the family doctor, who did blood tests and confirmed that it was ankylosing spondylitis, which, he explained, is a form of arthritis which gradually makes the spine rigid. Doctors are not fully aware whether it is hereditary or not, as it can miss generations only to reappear. It mostly affects men between the ages of fifteen and forty, although some women have been diagnosed in their later years. It was a cruel blow to Daniel, as he was anxious to make a career in the theatre, and had already made a good start. He wanted to be a director, but in view of my own experience I advised him to start as an assistant stage manager, as I had done. That way he would learn the whole business from the bottom upwards. He started as ASM with a touring musical, followed by some years with straight plays, musicals and pantos, but in 1983 he became too incapacitated to continue. In the summer of 1986 he had a hip replacement operation, and we hope the disease will either go into remission or burn itself out. He joined the Ankylosing Spondylitis Association, and through that, and through information given by specialists we realize that few doctors know much about it. The progress of spondylitis is so gradual that we have adjusted and learnt to cope with it, watching Daniel's walking become increasingly difficult over the years, while the pain hit him in cycles. Exercise is important for patients, who can help themselves a lot, but that is such an easy thing to say. It isn't so easy to be determined to help yourself when you're depressed and full of pain. We are sometimes told that we are never given a heavier burden that we can cope with. I believe we are tested, and that there is a reason for everything.

Certainly this must be true when I think of the circumstances which took me to Bath in February 1986 and the events which followed. I was in Shaw's *The Apple Cart*, which opened in Bath, and while we were there I was interviewed by a local journalist. I talked about Daniel's illness, and mentioned that I would have loved him to be treated in the Royal Mineral Hospital in Bath, but I knew how difficult it was to get a bed, unless one lived in the area or had a pressing recommendation from one's doctor. The article was published in the local paper on the Wednesday, and that night I had a call from the chief specialist at the Royal Mineral Hospital to say that there was a bed vacancy on the Friday if we wished to take advantage of it. I telephoned home with the good news, and Bill drove Daniel to Bath, where he went into hospital for four weeks of intensive physiotherapy and hydrotherapy. After he was discharged he came home for a few weeks before returning for his hip replacement operation, from which he slowly recuperated. Now Daniel is learning to live with this painful and restricting illness, and we pray for a cure.

Challenges can come from many directions, both in private and public life, when one is in the theatrical profession, and in 1968 came a real acting challenge in the form of a play by Ronald Millar called *They Don't Grow on Trees*, in which I had to play nine different parts. Seven of the characters were applicants for a job of cook-housekeeper to a composer and his wife. My changes of clothes and wigs had to be made with lightning speed, and at one point I had to change on stage behind a sofa. Inevitably, there came the moment when two of my characters were on stage at the same time, and we had to use a double. It was actually more fun backstage than on stage, but it was a frantic business, with wigs and clothes being flung on and off.

150

My dresser nearly had a nervous breakdown, and I think the play closed just in time.

My youngest son William was six when he saw the play in Manchester on its pre-London tour. When I came on in a black wig and mini-skirt as an Italian au pair, he announced in a loud voice for the whole audience to hear, 'I feel sick,' and had to be taken out. His mother's many other transformations were as Jessie — a Scots 'treasure'; Mrs Dawkins — a cockney char; Mrs Van Doren — a superior dragon; Brigid — an Irishwoman; Miss Minter — an impoverished gentlewoman; Mary Thornton — a shy mousey girl who was a blonde tearaway at night; Mrs Scully — a pleasant Lancashire lady; and Mrs Zuchmeyer — a wealthy American. My performances must have been convincing because Ronnie Millar and the director Val May were sure that I had played several characters before the audience realized that I was playing all the parts. So we decided the play could start with me as myself, telling the audience what was going to happen, then on stage dressing myself as the first character, the Scottish housekeeper who was leaving the household, thus setting the plot for the play. When I came on later as the lesbian lady with two dogs, a Dalmatian and a St Bernard, it became chaotic. The dogs were impossible to work with, barking hysterically in the wings, dragging me all around the stage, and growling at the audience. Actor Hugh Paddick and I had a lot of laughs — probably more than the audience — but after a few months we quietly closed, and I was very relieved. I was exhausted, and thought there had to be easier ways of making a living. There were — and although I was kept very busy during 1969 with a TV series, a summer season at Yarmouth, and a tour, it was still less tiring than making all those rapid changes of costume and character in *They Don't Grow on Trees*.

151

I then had a lot of fun doing Noel Coward's *Red Peppers* with Bruce Forsyth and the late Dame Edith Evans, for the BBC. The year ended with *The Dora Bryan Show* at the King's Theatre, Glasgow, with a young unknown and brilliant Freddie Starr. Also about this time I made a funny film with Frankie Howerd, *The Great St Trinian's Train Robbery*. I wasn't too sure about the red wig and weird clothes for my role of the headmistress, but I went up in my children's estimation when they saw the film. I didn't see it until it was shown on TV, and I loved it.

In 1970 I was invited to play Doll Common in *The Alchemist* at Chichester Festival Theatre. Suddenly I found myself making the transition from modern comedy and musicals to a Ben Jonson classic. Laurence Harvey was also cast in *The Alchemist*, in the role of Face, but as he was in another play he was unable to attend all the early rehearsals. A large four-poster bed features in the play, and instead of using a real bed at rehearsals we used a Dunlopillo mattress supported on chairs, which was very precarious. 'This is terribly dangerous,' I commented. 'Someone's going to break a leg.' One should never voice this sort of fear. It has a habit of encouraging a disaster. I arrived back from rehearsal to a telephone call, asking me if I could go back to Chichester for another rehearsal. It was explained to me that Laurence Harvey, who had followed me into rehearsal, was jumping around on the makeshift 'bed', and had fallen and broken a knee cap, which had put him completely out of action. His part was taken over by James Booth, but as he had only three days in which to learn it, director Peter Dews had to take over the role of Face on opening night, until James Booth knew it. On the whole, injuries are quite rare in our profession, but when they do occur they have to be fairly serious to keep an actor off the stage.

Although it is wonderful to have good press notices for performances, and publicity is all part and parcel of being in the entertainment business, it can be a two-edged sword. One has to take the good with the bad, and because I was well known, Clarges Hotel came in for a lot of media attention. Some years ago I was doing a pantomime in Bristol, and we rented a house there for the season. Clarges was happily fully booked over the Christmas period, and a firm called Templar's Catering Company asked us if we would be interested in leasing out the restaurant for a year, starting at Christmas. As many of the problems of running a hotel lie in the catering side, we were quite willing to do this, happy to think that we could safely leave that aspect in capable hands. When we had arrived at Clarges one of the first things we did was to close down the old basement kitchens and install new ones on the ground floor, with new equipment. The old kitchens were like dungeons, with ancient fittings, and old, impractical ovens. When the new kitchens were ready, the old ones in the basement were roped off and never used. We came to an agreement with the catering firm about a lease, and went off to spend Christmas in Bristol.

While we were away, the firm to whom we had leased the restaurant decided that it would be very convenient to make use of the extra ovens in the basement to cook the Christmas turkeys. That decision was our undoing. Somehow — and will we ever know how? — this news reached the ears of the local Health Inspector, who descended upon Clarges like the proverbial ton of bricks, with accusations about the kitchens being a health hazard. As owners of the establishment we were held responsible, even though we did not know it had happened and were miles away in Bristol at the time. Our statements that the old kitchens were extinct, had never been used by us, and that we wouldn't dream of using them, were all in vain. We were fined £3,000 in court, and the press had a field day. It showed the unpleasant side of fame, and because I was well known it was as though I had personally cooked those turkeys. The headlines were all about DORA BRYAN'S KITCHENS and DORA'S HOTEL. Of course I was upset, but it was like having a bad notice for a play, and one had to live with it for a time. Bill was more upset than I was. However innocent we were of the charge, it did not look good for the hotel. In addition to this, I received two poison-pen letters while I was in Bristol, indicating, each in its own objectionable way, 'Get out of Bristol. Go home and clean up your filthy kitchens.' It's sad that some people get a kick out of the misfortunes of others, or are compelled to turn to writing anonymous letters. I suppose people must be sick to do that kind of thing, and one should be understanding, but it isn't very easy to be charitable when you're on the receiving end of the letters.

Brighton has changed a lot now. It has almost ceased to be a regular holiday resort for families, who seem to be going abroad more and more. It has been taken over by the day trippers and the students, from this country and overseas. The commercial travellers, who were the hotelier's bread and butter, don't stay overnight any more. They have fast cars, and there are motorways which take them home quickly, or on to their next call. Business became bad in the Brighton hotel trade, and we started to lose money, so now Clarges is in the process of being turned into flats. We have had some happy times there, and I like to think we have made a lot of people happy. Certainly we have made some very good friends. We loved our staff, and were sad to see them go, but we did not have the heart to close the bar, which is run by Georgina and William, who have

154

17. Me as Doll Common with William Hutt in *The Alchemist* at Chichester.

18. With Les Dawson in *The Dora Bryan Show* at Blackpool.

19. At the Mandarin Hotel in Hong Kong with Eartha Kitt.

20. With Dawn Addams in Noël Coward's *Fallen Angels*.

21. On holiday in Malta with Joan Collins and Tony Newley.

22. Dougal, my best
dog.

23. The hotel and the
family, 1980.

worked in the hotel since leaving school. William left school at sixteen and started work there as trainee manager. Georgina made herself indispensable by learning all aspects of the work, and now she's very happy running the bar, and loves meeting the customers. Our regular customers are almost an extension of the family, and we are also popular with dog owners. No well-behaved dog is ever turned away, as long as the owner is well-behaved too.

We have made some interesting property purchases during our lives. We once went on an afternoon trip to have tea and visit a zoo, and we came back having bought a house, which might seem a little eccentric. When the children were young, if it was a dull day and we wanted to go out, we would sometimes make a visit to Alfriston, a charming place with a nice tea shop and a small zoo. One Sunday we were driving along the coast road towards Newhaven, and Bill turned off left. Within half a mile we were going through the village of Piddinghoe, which we had always admired. It looked as pretty as ever, and there, on a beautiful house on the river bank, was a 'FOR SALE' notice.

'Bill, let's go and look at it,' I urged. It was empty, and as we wandered around outside it the people from the next house along the river bank came running up to us with the keys. They told us they had built it themselves, complete with a granny annexe, but because of a bereavement they had decided to stay where they were. It was in such a wonderful position, and was a most unusual house, with a landing stage for our boat, which was moored at Newhaven. We all loved the house, and said we would let the owners know as soon as possible whether or not we would take it. Our thoughts and conversations were all about the house on the river while we walked around the zoo that afternoon, and had our cream tea. That night I found Georgina on her knees in her bedroom, praying that we could have the house. 'Georgina, we really mustn't pray for material things,' I admonished, managing to sound very shocked. But then I thought about that lovely house sitting there just waiting for us, and decided that perhaps it wouldn't be too wicked to help things along, so I was soon sending up a prayer with Georgina, quite sure that the house was meant for us anyway. I was opening at the London Palladium with Cliff Richard in a variety show the next day, and I didn't need to ask him to put in a good word for me with the Lord, as our prayers of the previous night were answered. Within a few weeks we moved in.

To have another five-bedroomed house only five miles away from our permanent home was sheer extravagance and not very practical, but we did enjoy our four years there. We swam in the river, watched the cows coming down to the river bank for an evening drink, saw the kingfishers skimming the water, and sometimes we would sail down the river to Newhaven with Daniel at the helm, tie up, and go shopping. Then we might get up early and take the children to Dieppe for the day on the big boats. What lovely school holidays we spent in those days!

The Juggs Arms was a delightful pub nearby, and as I had long been interested in the welfare of drug addicts, it was a great pleasure to see an old friend working there, looking healthy and happy, fully recovered from his addiction. We were also very pleased, if a little surprised, to be introduced to his girl friend. His friends had always seemed previously to be exclusively male, so we didn't think this could be a serious affair. We were wrong, because as the weeks went by the girl friend became increasingly plump, and it was obvious that she was pregnant. Eventually they had a beautiful baby boy, Timothy, but the responsibility of this was

156

something which Timothy's father could not cope with at all. He took an overdose and was rushed to hospital. Timothy's mother, poor girl, was desperately upset by this sudden turn of events, especially when she heard that her boy friend had disappeared from the hospital, and had not returned to her. She came to see me one evening at the house on the river, after the children had gone to bed. Bill was at our hotel in Brighton. She asked me if I could possibly have Timothy for the night, as she wanted to go and find his father. It seemed the least I could do, so I had no hesitation in agreeing to help. She went off, returning later with Timothy, and enough nappies and baby food to outlast a siege.

Timothy proved to be the most delightful little baby. He settled down in my bed as good as gold. When Bill arrived back from Brighton he found Timothy and me bedded down for the night, Timothy blissfully asleep, and me with a vaguely gooey expression on my face. It was nice to have another baby to cuddle.

'What's that?' asked Bill, pointing to the slumbering baby nestling beside me.

'It's not a That!' I replied indignantly. 'It's Timothy, and he's staying the night.'

Bill surveyed the pile of nappies and clothes, and the stack of tinned baby food with the utmost suspicion. 'Staying the night?' he echoed. 'What are you doing with all those nappies and clothes and food for one night?'

Bill was always more practical than I was, and although I had wondered the same thing it had never crossed my mind to question it. I should have done, because days went by with no sign of Timothy's mum, and it dawned on me that I really knew little or nothing about her. Neither did the Juggs Arms where she and Timothy's father had worked. Each day I thought I ought to telephone the police, but it seemed such a drastic thing to do. Anyway, I was so busy with Timothy, and secretly enjoying myself in spite of Bill's protests, that I didn't get around to that. More than a week went by, and I had to return to Brighton. We left a note on the door of the river house, in case Timothy's mother should return.

We had been back in Brighton for a few days when the doorbell rang, and there stood Timothy's mother, looking and acting as though she had just popped up to the shops for a loaf, having been away a couple of minutes. She collected the baby and left, and to this day we have never seen them again. By now Timothy will be in his teens.

The house at Piddinghoe eventually had to go, which was sad, but there came a time when I was busy, or away on tour, and the children didn't use it. Bill had to go to and fro to do the garden and keep it under control, so we had to admit that there was little point in keeping it. The crunch came when a disastrous fire destroyed the Palace Pier Hotel in Brighton, and the council began to tighten up on fire regulations throughout the town, with special attention paid to hotels and boarding houses. We found that we had to spend such an enormous amount on the hotel to conform with the very strict rulings about fire precautions that it seemed logical to dispose of the house on the river. It was the end of a very happy sequence in our lives. We did love that house.

The fire at the Palace Pier Hotel was particularly sad for me, as my friend Janet Cameron died as a result of it. I had been in rep with her many years ago, and when I went to see her in hospital, where she was being treated for what turned out to be fatal burns, she seemed to be only semi-conscious. I went up to her bed, which was a cot with sides on it. She lay there naked, and in a dreadful condition. I could hardly believe what I saw, and had to fight back the tears as I said quietly, 'It's Dora, Janet.'

There was a flicker of recognition, and the years fell away as she said, 'Dora Broadbent?'

'Yes.'

There weren't many who still thought of me by that name, but I'd known Janet for most of my life. That was the last time I saw her.

As an actress one is often asked to speak at various functions. I am nervous every time I accept. I'm usually expected to be amusing, so I was very worried about one speech I was asked to make as a guest of honour. It was at the Women of the Year lunch at the Savoy Hotel. This is an all-women occasion, and a very popular event, organized each year by the Marchioness of Lothian, and it raises a lot of money for the blind. The women guests of honour are all prominent in their own fields, and it's rather awe-inspiring. The topic we had to speak on that year was 'The Quality of Life', which I found very daunting, and the speech I had written seemed a bit heavy. I've got to get a laugh somehow, I thought. I was following an excellent speaker.

Most of the women at the lunch appeared to be of a certain age group, so I thought they might like to hear the one about the lady of their particular age group who was propositioned by a lovely young man at a party. She was delighted, and said she would love him to take her home, but she had to warn him that she was in her menopause. He replied that would be fine, as he would follow in his Mini-Cooper.

It got a nice laugh, and certainly lightened the rest of my speech on The Quality of Life. As I left to pick up my coat from the cloakroom, I heard Vivienne, the then royal photographer, say to her friend, 'I thought Dora Bryan was disgusting!' Oh dear. I sat on the loo and wept till everyone had gone. How fragile we actresses are at times.

159

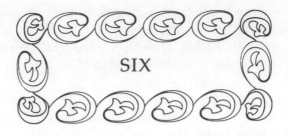

SIX

FAMILY HOLIDAYS WERE ALWAYS RATHER SPECIAL WHEN the children were young. I loved being in charge of them at those times, with no nanny. Few of our family trips were without incident, and there have been interesting journeys, unpleasant journeys, and absolutely disastrous journeys. Into this last category comes one made in Spain. In 1972 we set off in the Mercedes in high spirits, en route for two weeks' holiday at Jimmy and Pauline Tarbuck's villa in southern Spain. All went well on the way there, and we had a really good holiday. The villa, Chez Redez, was very comfortable, with everything one could wish for, and at the end of the holiday we left for the long journey home. We were to drive to Bilbao, where we would pick up the boat back to England.

I persuaded Bill to drive back via Granada so that the children could see the magnificent Moorish Palace (as if they cared). He was reluctant to make this detour, and was far more keen to take the shortest possible route, but I insisted upon this little cultural excursion, and he wasn't at all pleased. I don't really know why I bothered about taking in Moorish palaces, because the children were far more interested in their own private little domestic squabbles, and bickered constantly in the back of the car, as children are apt to do when a long journey becomes boring. To keep the peace I changed places with Daniel, and went into the back myself.

The road from Granada to Bilbao was like a snake. It was a narrow, twisting ribbon of a road as it wound its way round the mountains. Somewhere, for some inexplicable reason, I took special note of the time on a church clock. It was just one of those strange moments which imprint themselves on the mind. The church clock said ten minutes to four. We drove on for a short distance, and came to a particularly tricky stretch of road, where there was a sheer drop on our right. Driving conditions were far from ideal, and a slight drizzle of rain was falling. There was a patch of oil in the road, and we had an overloaded boot. I was aware of shouting, 'Bill, watch out . . .!'

Over we went, like taking off into the air. We landed on our side with a terrible sickening sound of broken glass and noise. Then came total silence. I knew I was badly hurt, but the silence was the worst thing of all. Then after an eternity of nothingness came the relief of hearing William crying, and Georgina's little voice saying plaintively, 'Daddy, I can't get out.' There was nothing from Bill or Daniel. I seemed to be swallowing glass. Then more blessed relief came as I heard Bill and Daniel talking quietly. That meant that at least everyone was alive. After what appeared to be hours, and amid the sound of subdued but urgent voices of people I didn't know, I was pulled out of the wrecked car by my feet.

The sight of my children at the side of the road was the most wonderful sight in the world at that moment. William was wearing a T-shirt with 'Kiss Kiss' written across the chest in red, but that was the only red in

161

sight. There was no blood on him. He was concussed, but alive. Georgina was shocked, but unhurt. Bill was safe, and Daniel had a cut eye, but was otherwise all right. The car was a complete wreck. As for me, I was shaking all over and seemed to be both numb and aching all at the same time. I just clung to Bill at the side of the road and tried to realize what an escape we had had. 'God has saved us,' was all I could manage to say in my state of shock.

Daniel and I were gently put into a little car and driven by some kind Spaniards to a clinic in Jaen, about thirty miles away. It was the longest drive I can ever remember. The pain was almost unbearable. When I caught sight of myself in a mirror at the clinic I was shocked at what I saw. My face was bleeding, my trousers were torn, and I was covered in grime and road dust. An examination showed that I had six broken ribs, and a broken collar bone and shoulder blade. Yet we were all so happy to be alive and together that somehow I felt I could cope with the pain. The worst thing was that we were so far from home, and no matter how kind people were, they were still strangers. At a time like that one longed for familiar faces and the security of home.

After X-rays and a few pills I was bedded down in a room with Georgina. Bill and the boys were accommodated somewhere else. During that first night the pain of all my broken bones and my bruised body was overpowering. I wakened Georgina and asked her to fetch a nurse, or anybody she could find. She got up and went in search, dressed for some reason in her bikini. I thought vaguely that this was a bit strange, but was in no mood to ask questions. All I wanted was for the awful pain to stop. After some time she returned, only to tell me, 'There's no one about anywhere.' In a clinic in Spain it seems that relatives nurse the sick! I

162

resigned myself to the aches and pains for the rest of the night.

The next day we were the centre of attention, not only because we were English, but because we could not pay the bill. All our travellers' cheques and money had been in the car with us, and everyone had been so concerned about getting us out of the wreckage that little matters like travellers' cheques had not entered anyone's head. All the visiting relatives of the other patients made a great fuss of us, and showered us with food — mainly lettuce. They were lovely, and their lettuce was very nice, but nothing altered the fact that we did not have enough money with us to pay the bill at the clinic. As nobody spoke English it was very difficult for us to get the message across that we were highly respectable and wouldn't dream of not paying a bill. Our only hope was the British Embassy in Madrid. It was a Saturday morning, and most of the staff were off duty, so when Bill telephoned the embassy we were faced with the unbelievable situation of finding an embassy employee who didn't speak Spanish! As he wouldn't have been much use for translating our predicament we were no better off, except that any kind of communication from the British Embassy probably carried more conviction than we did. The embassy official went through the same routine that we had already been through, and with great difficulty managed to convey to the people at the clinic that the embassy would meet the bill.

So we were released, I being strapped up in all relevant places, to hold together my broken bones. As we set out in a taxi for Madrid we looked like a family of refugees. My agent in England had made all the arrangements for us to fly home from Madrid.

We sank back into the taxi with sighs of relief. Thank God we were going home at last. We were still shaken by everything that had happened to us during the past forty-eight hours. After a few miles in the taxi, bouncing along the uneven road, we had the misfortune to witness another accident. Two cars had a head-on collision. It was all too much for me. The two cars burst into flames and I burst into tears. 'No further, please!' I begged weepily. I just could not have driven another mile along that road. The taxi driver found us a Parador where they spoke English, agreed very kindly to take an English cheque, and undertook to get a doctor for me. I fell thankfully into bed, and a large, beautifully dressed Spanish doctor arrived, accompanied by another gentleman plus a long needle and a syringe. In went the needle, and I had a few blissful hours free from pain. The next day we set off again, with me still feeling very sore and aching, wishing we were home again without having to travel there. Our confidence had been restored a little, but we weren't entirely convinced that, in Spain at least, there was much hope of keeping death off the road. This time we only made a short gentle taxi trip to the little local railway station, where we took a slow — very slow — train to Madrid.

Again we were the centre of attention during the journey and more food and wine was pressed upon us. We all looked very pathetic — me, particularly. I was still in my torn trousers, and not very clean. The kind Spanish doctors had given me something in a phial to ward off the pain, but as I wasn't sure whether I was expected to drink it or inject it, I decided to do neither. After six long hours on that train there came the flight back to England. Oh, the blessed relief of being back on home ground! I turned down the offer of a wheelchair at the airport. We took a taxi to Victoria and caught the first available train back to Brighton, where my sister-in-law Adah was waiting, and Dr Weir was there with his injections. I accepted them gratefully in the comfort of my own bed.

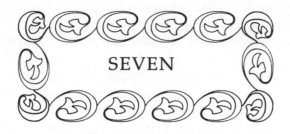

SEVEN

I'VE WORKED WITH SOME WONDERFUL PEOPLE IN SHOW business and one of my favourites is Larry Grayson, who is a good friend. We both like to chat on a telephone, and sometimes we talk for ages. If we are working near each other we always meet, and manage to make each other laugh. We seem to spark off a chain of amusing stories and anecdotes.

I first saw Larry in a summer show at the Theatre Royal, Brighton. He was completely unknown to me, and the theatre was only about a third full — mostly with old age pensioners. He walked on, immaculately dressed, carrying a bentwood chair, which he placed near the microphone. He leaned on the chair, flicked an imaginary piece of dust from his suit, and said to the audience, confidentially, 'This theatre's filthy. And they've got Ingrid coming next week. Hope to God they clean it up for her.' Ingrid Bergman was coming the following week in *Captain Brassbound's Conversion*. I loved Larry Grayson from that moment, and rocked in my seat. I had taken the children to see the show, and they kept telling me to shut up. I seemed to be the only member of the small audience who was laughing. As I was going to be in pantomime at this same theatre at Christmas (and I must add that it's perfectly clean, of course!), I made sure this wonderful man was in it with me.

The pantomime was *Goldilocks and the Three Bears*, and we had a lot of fun together. We gave a special matinée for some mentally sub-normal patients from a local hospital, whom I found very bright. Usually, when we reached the spot in the pantomime when I said to the audience, 'I've lost Goldilocks. What shall I do?' there would be an audience response from the children: 'She's in the woods with the bears.' But on the day we gave our special performance there was quite a different reaction. A lady stood up, and in a charmingly refined voice she helpfully informed me, 'She's gone back to her changing room, Dora.'

One poor man in the front row moaned loudly every time the bears made an appearance. His friend, obviously in charge of him, would tap him sharply on the face to silence him. After the performance the audience wanted to meet us all in the stalls, and particularly wanted to meet the bears. The trouble was that the actors playing the bears had become very hot in their skins, and removed them as quickly as possible so that they could rush out for tea. There was great disappointment that there were no bears available, but Larry Grayson dealt with that situation. He told the bears' fans that Baby Bear was drunk, and Mummy and Daddy Bear were looking after her. Everyone thought that was a perfectly reasonable explanation.

You can get away with a lot in pantomime. I remember one Cinderella being played by a member of Ivy Benson's All Girl Band. She was sitting in her rags by the fireplace, unable to go to the ball. The dialogue went like this: 'Hey ho! I'm sad, forlorn, and all alone. I know — I'll play my saxophone . . .' Whereupon she picked up a saxophone from the fireplace and played 'I'm in the Mood for Love'. Another equally daft scene was in *Robinson Crusoe*. It was an underwater scene, with mermaids and fishes swimming by, and seashells and seaweed for good measure. One of the characters, Billy, walked in wearing full evening dress singing, 'Here on the floor of the ocean bed, King Neptune reigns quite supreme . . .' At this, two stage hands, not very well disguised as mermen, wheeled on a grand piano, and Billy played his latest medley.

There's quite often a trampoline act, and a few acrobats in the woodland scene before Goldilocks appears looking for her bears. The audience takes it as quite normal. When I was appearing at home in Brighton with Larry in *Goldilocks*, my children, who were young then, came often, and knew the script well. So well did they know it that when I had to say to the audience, 'Oh dear, I am so poor that I shall have to sell the bears,' the audience would normally cry, 'No, Dora! Don't sell them!' But my own children shouted, 'Go on, Dora! You sell them. They smell!' I could have killed whichever one it was.

During the last week of the run in Brighton all the children had gone back to school after the holidays, so the matinée audiences were full of pensioners. I walked on stage for my opening chat, and caught the eye of the only child in the audience, in the third row. It was Justin, a friend of my children. I was so surprised that I came right out of character as Dame Dora Dolittle, and said, 'Justin, why aren't you at school?' Justin sprang to attention and replied. 'Well, Mrs Lawton, I had a bad cold last week and couldn't come, so Mrs Watkins (his headmistress) said I could have the afternoon off to come today.' So much for the magic of stage illusion, but somehow in pantomime it just doesn't seem to destroy the magic, and sometimes adds to the friendly

167

atmosphere. Pantomime is like a glorious party.

That pantomime was in 1972, but in 1973, six months after the car accident, I started to have really bad depressions, and had to have treatment. Apart from the time when I lost my first baby and there was an obvious reason for it, I had never felt so low. And this time it seemed to be different; it was almost melancholia, and there was nothing I could do about it. From being a happy, bubbly, talkative human being I became introverted, unsure of myself. My confidence simply drained away. Bill was very worried about me, but the doctor assured him that it was delayed shock after the accident. Anti-depressants were prescribed, and after the show I would have a few drinks to try and cheer myself up. For some reason nobody had seen fit to warn me of the consequences and danger of drinking even a small amount of alcohol when on the course of pills. The result was that there was little or no improvement in my condition. When I was working I felt better, but the despair would always come back when I stopped. I tried hard in front of the children to be my old self, but the situation dragged on for some years. At times I managed to cope, but at other times the depressions were quite overwhelming. A doctor in Blackpool said it was 'my age', and I'd have to put up with it.

After the pantomime and our usual family Easter holiday, I had a twelve-week summer season in Blackpool with *The Dora Bryan Show* again. It was the time we rented the house with the ducks. This time the season was with Les Dawson, Lennie Bennett and Ronnie Hilton. We had a great season and were the last show to play at the lovely Queen's Theatre. Now it's a Marks and Spencer's (who else?). I soon realized that although I'd never seen Les Dawson on stage before, we were all going to see a lot of him in the future. A very clever and funny man. We did a sketch as a very

168

Northern, very shy honeymoon couple, preparing for their first night together. After sitting on the bed and discussing honeymoons, we eventually undressed and got into bed, me still with my hat on. After Les made a grab at me to try and kiss me, the bed would collapse, with enormous laughs from the audience. My last line was, 'My Mum said honeymoons was always a bit of a let down.' Stage blackout.

One night we walked on stage, sat on the bed, and to our astonishment it collapsed before we'd started. The audience laughed just as loudly, but we were ever so cross. It did ruin the sketch.

I then had to cut my Blackpool act down to fifteen minutes so that I could fit it into Cliff Richard's season at the London Palladium, which also included the Shadows and Olivia Newton John. This show was Olivia's first stage show as a solo artist. She was a delightful, fresh young lady, who came to my dressing room one day and said, 'Dora, what's all this religious stuff that goes on backstage?' I must say that I was amazed, and thought Cliff must be very special to be able to cope with all the young Born Again Christians who came to see him, filling his dressing room each night. I would have found it very distracting — but then he would have found it equally distracting trying to cope with a dressing room full of children and dogs.

It was a great boost to be invited to appear at the Hong Kong Festival in 1973, and was probably the best tonic I could possibly have had. The engagement was at the Mandarin Hotel, which is one of the best in the world, and my delight at being invited was tempered with fear. I just had to have a good act to impress that particular audience, which was very sophisticated and used to some of the world's best cabaret artists. I had already made a promise to Oldham Rep that I would do two weeks for them in a play, and that was booked

before the Hong Kong invitation arrived, so I suggested
we did a revue at Oldham. I would do the first half of
the show with the resident company, and in the second
half I would do forty-five minutes by myself. This solo
performance would then form the basis of the show I
would take to Hong Kong, and would be well polished
by the time I reached the Mandarin Hotel. As always,
my home town of Oldham was friendly, full of warmth,
and that very good director, the late Carl Paulsen was
extremely helpful in co-operating with me in putting
the act together. The first half of the show proved to be
great fun, with the members of the rep company and
me doing sketches from the various revues I had
been in over the years. One member of the cast at that
time was Anne Kirkbride from *Coronation Street*, and
Judith Barker and her husband Kenneth Allon Taylor
were also in it.

We had a really good show, which was very successful, and then Bill and I left for Hong Kong. Oh, the
glamour of it all! The contrast of landing in the Far East,
having just left Oldham, was like some sort of dream,
especially as we were met at the airport by a white Rolls
Royce — they didn't go in for that kind of reception at
Oldham Rep. Our hotel suite overlooked the Hong
Kong cricket ground, and we loved watching the ferries
going back and forth to Kowloon. The floating restaurants were fascinating, and the shops in the hotel
were beautiful. It was all strangely unreal. We had two
days in which to recover from our jet lag, and ate in all
five of the hotel's restaurants.

Eartha Kitt was already appearing in cabaret at the
hotel, and we were invited to her last performance. Of
course she was wonderful, and knowing that I was
going to follow her on that stage the following night
was enough to produce not only butterflies in my
stomach, but a fluttering collection of Chinese moths as

170

24. With Moira Lister, Peter O'Toole, Paul Rogers, David Waller, Michael Denison and Geoffrey Keen in *The Apple Cart*.

25. At the National Theatre as Mrs Hardcastle with Tom Baker in *She Stoops to Conquer*.

26. *Charlie Girl* at the Victoria Palace, 1986. Nicholas Parsons, me, Paul Nicholas, Cyd Charisse and Mark Wynter.

well. We were invited to her suite after the show, and Miss Kitt entertained everyone lavishly with champagne — bottles and bottles of Dom Perignon seemed to be circulating. This must be the way to behave when you're a cabaret star, I thought; champagne for everyone. I mentally filed the information for future use. Eartha Kitt was going on to Ringmer, near Lewes in Sussex for her next engagement, so I gave her the keys of our lovely river house in Piddinghoe, which was quite near, and invited her to stay there with her daughter Kitt, who was with her in Hong Kong. She was delighted, and they spent a few relaxing weeks there. I count her as a friend, and am always pleased to see her when she's in England. A most intelligent lady, and a wonderful artist. She was certainly a hard act to follow at the Harbour Room in Hong Kong, but when it comes to the point, however apprehensive we may be, we just have to get up there and get on with it, which I did the next night. I need not have worried, as I was given a tremendous reception, which came as a great relief, and stilled the internal butterflies and moths.

As I stood there on the stage, looking out at all the twinkling lights across the river, and listening to the applause, I couldn't help thinking that Oldham and Hong Kong weren't any different really. I just wished my mum could have been there to share it all with me. But I had Bill, who did a marvellous job as my stage manager, dresser and lighting expert, which was very commendable for an ex-cricketer and hotelier! As it was the season of the Hong Kong Festival, all the important residents and visitors came to my show, and I thought the time had come to hand round the champagne, just as Eartha Kitt had done. I had taken the precaution of ordering six bottles of Dom Perignon for the purpose of entertaining, and was quite prepared to go on doing so for the duration of my show, but the managing director fortunately stepped in and put me right before I spent my entire salary on champagne. 'You don't have to do this every night,' he said. 'It was written into Eartha Kitt's contract that she was supplied with champagne — one bottle each night to be used during her show, and one for entertainment purposes.' Well, that explained a lot, and at least it meant that I'd have money left to do some shopping and buy presents for the family at home.

I had for some time been involved with a 'Life for the World' project, which had a rehabilitation centre for drug addicts at Northwick Park in Gloucestershire. It was run on a spiritual basis by a committed friend of ours, the Reverend Frank Wilson. We had given holidays to some of his boys at our hotel in Brighton, and tried to help in any way we could. I had met a Chinese boy at his centre and had said to him, 'If we ever come to Hong Kong we'll look you up.' It was one of those things one says without really thinking, and certainly at the time I had never dreamed I would ever go to Hong Kong. But there I was, and I thought it would be nice to keep my word and look up Henry Chan, who wasn't an addict himself, but had been at Northwick Park to see how it compared with their centre in Longkair, on the borders of Red China.

Attempting to find Henry Chan in the Hong Kong telephone directory is like looking for John Smith in England, but with the help of an English reporter I was put on the right track. I found Jackie Pullinger, an English girl working with drug addicts in the Walled City. We had been offered the use of a police launch for a day to go anywhere we wished, so Bill and I, with Jackie and some of her friends, splashed all the way to Longkair, passing all the junks and Chinese fishing trawlers as we sped along. We had the most wonderful, and very moving day at the centre, and met all the

172

resident ex-addicts. They were a completely self-supporting community, kept chickens and goats, and had built a little chapel. It was tremendously uplifting, and if ever I had reason to doubt my already strong faith I could never doubt it again. From being hardened heroin addicts and members of the dreaded gangs in the Walled City, here they were, living proof of a living faith. The Governor of Hong Kong had offered to send a doctor to help them, but they had declined and had said that Jesus was helping them, and that was all they needed. They were prayed through their horrific withdrawal symptoms with no medical help at all. Miraculous. Jackie became a great friend, and I love to see her when she comes to England to lecture, or to speak on TV about her work.

It's amazing the friends you meet a long way from home. On our return from Longkair to Hong Kong island, after that uplifting day I fell asleep on a bunk in the police launch. As we pulled in along the quayside I opened my eyes, looked out of the porthole, and saw the name *HMS Brighton*. The last time we had seen her was at anchor in the English Channel, opposite our house on the sea front at Brighton. We had been entertained on board then, and were entertained on board again that night in Hong Kong.

In Brighton we had been asked to board the ship, as we had been circling around her in our little cabin cruiser. The children and I had clambered up a ladder, leaving Bill to carry on circling and, of course, using up valuable fuel. No one thought to tie him up to the ladder. The children and I had a lovely time touring the ship. Bill was furious with me as he went round in circles. We had to get back to our house on the river at Piddinghoe, near Newhaven, where we moored the boat. We said our goodbyes, and climbed aboard our little boat. It was getting dark as we passed the menacing looking cliffs at Peacehaven, and fuel was very low. I had implored the children to pray hard, and we just made it to Newhaven.

Now there was a ship that had entertained us in the Channel offering us hospitality again in Hong Kong! Yes, Hong Kong was a great experience in many different ways, but as always, I was looking forward to going home. The London Philharmonic Orchestra had been playing at the Hong Kong Festival, and we all travelled back together on the plane. They were very doubtful about the Chinese method of stowage, and refused to trust their precious musical instruments in the aircraft luggage hold, so it was all rather crowded when we were installed, complete with a collection of cellos and double basses and large brass instruments. I didn't care where my stuff went. I just couldn't wait to get home with my mountains of presents for everyone.

Bill and I had met Mr and Mrs Bunny Austin when they were on holiday in Brighton. Bunny was the famous Wimbledon tennis champion, and his wife, Phyllis Konstam, had been an actress before they were married. Through Bunny I was introduced to Moral Rearmament, and was asked to do a play for them at the Westminster Theatre. The plays performed there are usually plays and musicals with a Christian message. This was a play about drug addicts and a priest. I was to play the mother of an addict. The play was also being performed at Moral Rearmament's centre, a castle which is run as a hotel in Caux, in Switzerland. Caux is a wonderful place to visit, a real beauty spot overlooking the lake at Montreux. Moral Rearmament held conferences there, aiming to create goodwill between different nationalities. I decided to see for myself what the play was like, and as it was a half term school holiday, I took Georgina with me. She was about fourteen at the time.

174

They were holding an Arts Conference at the castle at the time, and gave a Saturday morning performance of the play especially for us. The author, Georgina and I, and a few other visitors, watched the play, which was rather long and gloomy. I wondered what on earth I could say about it to the author at the interval. We went out into the sunshine for a drink at the little station café overlooking the mountains, and Georgina said everything for me: 'Mummy, is it a bad play, or are they bad actors?' The author was a very nice man, and pretended he hadn't heard. Needless to say, I did not do the play at the Westminster Theatre. Yet the Caux centre was a wonderful place where everyone helped each other. It was rather like an up-market holiday camp, but much more sedate, and with a lot of goodwill towards all the different people of varied cultures who were staying there. Guests were expected to wait at tables and do a little plain cooking from the menus and recipes which were written out for reference.

While I was there I remembered that I had Noël Coward's Swiss address and telephone number with me. He lived at Les Avants, and I didn't realize it was just a few miles away. We felt a change of atmosphere would be a relief, so I telephoned. Noël was away, but Graham Payn, an old friend of mine from the days of the Lyric and Globe revues, was there with Cole Lesley, Noël's secretary. They were delighted to hear from us, and Graham sent the white MG sports car for us. Off we drove across the mountain, and had a truly sophisticated evening — smoked salmon, champagne, and lots of laughter and music in Noël's Swiss Cottage, as he called it. Graham said they were quite used to people phoning from Caux and saying, 'Help!'

However, I had been very impressed with Caux, and thought the whole family could do with a bit of this Christian way of life. So I decided that on our next

175

holiday we would all go. This, I must admit, was an error of judgement.

Daniel was hitch-hiking through France, and had said he would meet us in Caux for Georgina's birthday. We never for a moment thought he would make it, or even find the place. But 29 August came, and we were having our morning coffee at the station café. It was a beautiful sunny day, and we had said our birthday greetings and had given Georgina her presents. As we watched we saw the little train climbing the mountain, and who should be leaning out of the window but Daniel, shouting, 'Happy birthday!' He had spent all her birthday money, which had been given to him to pass on to her by relatives at home, but we didn't care.

We introduced him to Caux, but it was definitely not his scene. He called the place 'Colditz'. Discos were more in Daniel's line, and he was very unpopular in his leather and his cowboy boots. It wasn't appreciated either when he arrived back at Caux after a late night in Montreux, having taken the twelve-year-old son of an African diplomat. A big mistake. We were not a popular family. Bill enjoyed meeting Conrad Hunt, the West Indian cricketer who was there, and was working full time for Moral Rearmament, and we did celebrate Georgina's birthday at the little station restaurant. It at least had a juke box, so we all lived it up a little that night.

Some years after the first trip to Hong Kong I made a return visit, with the play *Shut Your Eyes and Think of England* (which I did frequently!). Andrew Sachs, Derek Bond and Alan Cuthbertson were in the cast, and we all loved the trip. I missed having Bill with me this time, but took Georgina and William. Another member of the cast was Anna Dawson, and Jackie Pullinger took us on a visit to the Walled City. It was unbelievable, with tiny narrow dark alleyways, open sewers, rats, and child

176

prostitutes. Amid all this squalor everyone seemed to know Jackie, as she had opened a youth club there, and was greatly respected. She has written about all her experiences in her book *Chasing the Dragon*, and she's a wonderful girl, with a shining faith and tremendous courage.

Having Georgina and William with me was hair-raising in more ways than one, as Hong Kong can be a very strange place. They also spent my entire salary, because the shops completely went to their heads, just as they had gone to mine on my first visit. In view of my own spendthrift tendencies I could hardly complain, and we all had a lovely time. Then it was back to earth, and a return to the English theatre, playing the role of Gwenny in *The Late Christopher Bean* at Watford, and later at Worthing.

Work had continued to come in before my second trip to Hong Kong, and in 1977 I did a tour with Dawn Addams of *Fallen Angels*, a delightful Noël Coward play, and very funny. Noël always maintained he could never find two suitable actresses to play the leading roles. He thought they had finally been found when Hermione Gingold and Hermione Baddeley played the parts, but when he saw the performance by these two larger-than-life characters he was absolutely furious about their interpretations, thinking they had gone completely 'over the top'.

Ours was a long tour of twelve weeks, and as Dawn did not learn lines very quickly I had her to stay with us in Brighton so that we could spend some time on it together. I'm a great believer in knowing the words so well that no matter what goes wrong on stage the words will come out, and the play will keep moving along. In due course we set out on tour. At the time Dawn was writing her life story. We shared digs and hotels together, and I was reading chapters as she wrote them.

After two marriages, the first to Michael Howard, and the second to Prince Vittorio Massimo, she was then happily married to a charming man called Jimmy White, who accompanied us on tour for a couple of weeks. Our tour ended with two weeks on my home ground, Oldham Repertory Theatre. It wasn't the best time to be there, as it happened to be Wakes Week, when a lot of the population takes an annual holiday, so many of those who would normally have been in the audience were out of town. But, as always, it was a joy to be playing at Oldham again. I stayed with my sister-in-law, Nellie, and Dawn stayed at the pub opposite the theatre. It was one of those rare, very hot English summers, and Dawn and I sunbathed in Nellie's backyard. Dawn would take a taxi to Nellie's each day, where, behind her two-up and two-down house, with Asians and Pakistanis on either side, and a mosque opposite, Nellie had magically created a flower-decked patio with hanging baskets and deck chairs. Dawn and I would bask contentedly there. With a bottle of wine between us and blue skies overhead we imagined we were in the South of France instead of Oldham, with its chimneys and industry. I would sometimes look around and think how strange it was that I was sitting there with an ex-princess. Sadly, that lively, lovely princess died of cancer in 1985. Later I was to do *Fallen Angels* with two other partners — Liz Fraser and Hildegarde Neil.

My depressions started to lift slightly in 1978 because there was so much to do, and I was kept busy. There was a production of *Mrs Warren's Profession* for the Brighton Festival, at the Gardner Theatre, which was an excellent production and worthy of a London showing, but in spite of our hopes to take it into the West End we couldn't do so. My emotional see-saw continued, and I was really low when I played Mrs Leverett in *Rookery*

178

Nook in 1979 at Her Majesty's Theatre. I dreaded going to the theatre and I dreaded going on stage. I was convinced that I was going to forget my lines and 'dry' in the middle of a performance. It was no comfort to me at all to be told that even Sir Laurence Olivier at one point in his career suffered from the most agonizing stage fright. I never told anyone at the theatre how I felt. I'm sure that had I done so I would have received understanding and sympathy, but as an experienced actress I was ashamed to have such fears, and felt I would be letting people down. By the time the play ended I was really ill, but committed to a big musical, *On the 20th Century*, in which there was a marvellous part for me. It too was being put on at Her Majesty's Theatre, produced by Harold Fielding. I rehearsed for just one week, if it could be called rehearsing. My heart simply wasn't in it. I felt dreadful, and couldn't wait to get home every night, back to Bill, back to the security, to escape into sleep with the aid of what had become my nightly dose of pills. I had no idea what was wrong. All I knew was that there was no way in which I could do that musical. My doctor visited me, and I was taken into a nursing home for treatment. The theatre management had to be told I could not continue. I did not know at the time, but apparently they waited hopefully until the last minute before re-casting the part. Oh, the guilt I felt when I learned this. The gloom which had settled upon me during *Rookery Nook* I had hugged to myself. It was all mine, and no one must know that there was anything wrong with me, while in fact I was just about hanging on to my sanity.

After my collapse I had six weeks of complete sedation and electro-convulsive therapy, which is a recognized treatment for depression. A low amperage electric current is passed between two electrodes placed on the side of the head, and causes small 'shocks'. At no time during all this treatment did anyone ask me about my drinking habits, so I had no reason to think my breakdown had anything to do with it. But I had noticed, and so had Bill, that even the smallest amount of alcohol could affect me very quickly indeed. I realized it was bad for me, and that all drinking had to stop. I never mentioned this to the doctors, but it was beginning to prey on my mind that perhaps I had a drinking problem, quite apart from my depressive illness.

I felt that I had to talk to someone about this, so I called my best friend, who had moved to Bournemouth, and had at one time coped with the same problem herself. Many a bottle of champagne or a stiff Martini we had shared together when we were younger, but she now had several years of sobriety behind her. She had always told me that I was in no danger of having such a problem because I never let drinking interfere with my work. She sent a friend of hers to see me. I don't remember what was said on that first visit because I was still in the nursing home and full of drugs, but she kept coming to see me, and I shall be for ever grateful for the friendship and understanding she gave me. When I had recovered I told my doctor that I had stopped drinking entirely. According to him, my breakdown had nothing whatever to do with any drinking I may have been doing, but how glad I am that I was led to take some action about it. Life completely without alcohol is certainly much better for me. At one time it seemed unthinkable that an actor or actress could survive without the occasional relaxing drink, and I had assumed that because I drank after the show, they all did. Yet I have discovered that I am not the odd one out. Many members of our profession don't drink.

When I felt well enough, Bill and I went off to Majorca, leaving the family to look after my beloved dogs. Before we went I took the drastic action of throwing all my pills down the loo. I felt strong enough to cope without them. This was probably a great mistake, because after all the sedation to which I had become accustomed I suddenly found a new lease of life. It was as though I had been walking around only half awake, and now my energy and non-stop chatter absolutely wore Bill out. I was living on a constant 'high', but anything was better than the way I had been.

After our return from Majorca my agent phoned and asked me to do a long tour of *The Cure for Love* with Christopher Timothy, Carol Drinkwater and Carmen Silvera. I was to play the role Gladys Henson had played in the film all those years previously. I still wasn't completely fit, and was unable to relax. It must have been very wearing for the rest of the company, but the excess energy enabled me to knit a great many sweaters for Georgina, and my little dog Dougal had lots of exercise. It was a very successful and happy tour. Then Daniel and I went off to Zimbabwe for a panto-mime together, Daniel being stage manager, as his illness wasn't disabling at that point. The pantomime was *Babes in the Wood*, which we naturally soon re-named *Babes in the Bush*. I was very homesick for Bill and the rest of the family, but Daniel was a great comfort, and we became very close. He was an excellent stage manager, and always treated me on a professional basis in the theatre, referring to me as 'Miss Bryan' and not 'Mum', although he did forget himself on one occasion when I missed an entrance. It wasn't his fault. I was doing a quick change in my dressing room when he called over the inter-com, 'Miss Bryan, two minutes please'. Then it was, 'Miss Bryan, one minute please. . . . .' His voice became panic-stricken. 'Miss Bryan. . . . .MUM! You're off!'

Zimbabwe was thousands of feet above sea level, and on stage it was sometimes hard to take the deep breaths necessary for the songs and dancing. One night at the beginning of the run I happened to say, 'Oh, I can't breathe.'

'You need oxygen,' I was told.

Next night there were some enormous cylinders in my dressing room, and I wondered what on earth they were there for. 'You said you needed it,' said one of the stage staff.

'I just meant I needed *air*,' I replied, very ungratefully. 'I don't know how to use these tank things.'

Although I survived without them, I must say that oxygen cylinders had their place while playing in Zimbabwe. The first time I had seen them in use was in London, of all places, by skating star Sonja Henie, who had them in her dressing room during the making of her film *Sonja Henie in London*, which was made for television, and in which I had a part. I'd seen her Hollywood films, of course, and was surprised to meet this doll-like person, rather like a little girl, wearing puffed-sleeve dresses and white Peter Pan collars. On the ice she made a spectacular picture in that show, as the ice was black, and she was dressed all in white. It brought back memories of watching her at the local cinema when I was a youngster, and being so fired with ambition to skate 'like Sonja Henie' that I was bought a pair of ice skates. At that time I didn't ever expect to meet her in London. That was just one of life's unexpected bonuses, for we never know what's around the next corner.

That great musical *Gypsy* was around the corner in 1981, at the Connaught Theatre, Worthing. This was a tremendous challenge, as it had to be put together in three weeks. I went to Majorca and learnt it out at sea, because all the numbers were big 'bashy' numbers and

I needed to get away from everyone to practise. I have always found great difficulty in singing quietly any-way, so this was a wonderful way to rehearse. I could let rip, and not disturb anybody — except the fish. We played to packed houses with *Gypsy* and it was a great success.

Apart from playing the small part of Bianca in *Othello* at Oldham Rep, I had not played any Shakespearean roles, so it was a thrill to be asked to play Mistress Quickly in *The Merry Wives of Windsor* at Regent's Park Open Air Theatre in the summer of 1984. I went to see managing director David Conville, and we had a picnic on the lawns outside the theatre while we discussed matters. It was the most unusual, and one of the pleasantest, theatrical discussions I have ever had, sitting out on the grass on a lovely day, instead of in a stuffy office. I knew Ronald Fraser, who was going to play Falstaff in the production, and I also knew that he would be very good in the role. Kate O'Mara was to play Mistress Ford, and Phillipa Gail was to be Mistress Page. I felt rather in awe of these experienced Shakespearean actors during rehearsals, but learned later that they were in awe of me. That surprised me, especially as it had been forty-four years since I had had anything to do with Shakespeare.

I loved playing in the park, and walking through the beautiful formal gardens to go to the theatre every evening. It rained on our opening night, and as I stood in the wings, which in Regent's Park are living trees and bushes, a little squirrel ran over my foot. I couldn't believe it. That was nice, and something that doesn't happen on the average opening night, but the Regent's Park squirrels are delightfully tame little animals, and the visitors feed them. Fortunately, the first night rain wasn't enough to stop the performance, and we simply carried on. The audience at the park are a pretty hardy

183

lot, and seem to take all the elements in their stride. One or two umbrellas went up in the back rows, and other people put newspapers over their heads, refusing to let the steady drizzle disturb their pleasure. There were drips of rain constantly forming on my nose, my wig was wet, and my Mistress Quickly dress was beginning to feel a bit damp, but I didn't mind at all, and it was a useful coincidence that Mistress Quickly did not have to be immaculate in her attire. We all forged ahead and completed the performance. Next day I had some lovely notices, and was particularly proud of the one which praised my interpretation of the part and said, 'Trevor Nunn and Peter Hall, take note . . .' The critics weren't used to seeing me in Shakespeare, so I had been rather nervous of their reactions.

For the final performances the production was taken to the beautiful setting of Arundel Castle, where a false stage had been built up in front of the battlements. The last scene of the play is supposed to be in the woods, and the little fairies all came down with their torches. There happened to be a full moon, and the whole atmosphere was sheer magic. I had never had such a perfect theatrical experience. I would gladly do another season in the park, even if there is no chance of actors growing fat on the salaries. The Regent's Park Open Air Theatre is for actors who simply love acting for the sake of it, and it was a memorable summer.

As a result of playing Mistress Quickly, I was invited to play Mrs Hardcastle in *She Stoops to Conquer* at the National Theatre in 1985, and I was both honoured and delighted to accept. It was a wonderful part for me, and in addition to being a rewarding role to play, it gained me two awards; the Variety Club of Great Britain award, and the *Manchester Evening News* award for the best visiting actress to the city. Glenda Jackson, Maggie Smith and Sue Pollard were the other nominees. We had visited Manchester during the National Theatre tour and played at the Palace Theatre, which for me was like going back home. Not only had I played there in *Hello, Dolly!* some years ago, but it was also the theatre where I had made my very first professional stage appearance as an excited little Drury Lane Babe. It was as though life had gone full circle, and that theatre holds many memories for me. When we were appearing there as children we were never allowed to use the lifts, presumably in case anything went wrong and we were stuck in them. It's a rambly old place backstage, and I could never remember where the stairs were. Perhaps I wasn't trying very hard, or perhaps I was too busy thinking of other things when I was twelve years old. I distinctly remember the night my friend Vera Swindells and I encountered a rat on the stairs. That is one recollection which has never left me!

It was a strange feeling, fifty years later, to be sitting in that dressing room recalling the twelve-year-old, who somehow seemed to have nothing to do with me. The little girl in the frilly dress, with the white socks and tap shoes, who kept losing her way backstage and was scared stiff of the rat on the stairs was like somebody else entirely. How could it happen that half a century later I should be brought back to exactly the same place, clad in period dress, with wig and beauty spot, waiting to go on as Mrs Hardcastle to speak Oliver Goldsmith's language? So much had happened in those fifty years. Life had changed and moved on, and yet there is nothing like an old theatre for inspiring a sense of nostalgia. It seemed particularly apt that I should be fortunate enough to have an award come my way for my performance in Manchester that year. It was almost like an anniversary present, and it meant a lot. Then out of the blue came a letter from the Variety Club of Great Britain, inviting me to attend one of their lunches as I

185

had been nominated — again with Glenda Jackson and Maggie Smith — as Best Actress of the Year (1985). I was so pleased to go and collect my Silver Heart award because it is given by businessmen who love the theatre and who also do a lot of charity work for children. They give a great deal of pleasure to a lot of people, including those who receive awards.

It was a wonderful experience to play in the National Theatre company, but I found great difficulty in becoming accustomed to the National Theatre building; to me, it was like a block of offices. When I'd been successful in finding the stage I never wanted to leave it, because once I was out in that maze of corridors I felt I was back in the office block again, and not in a theatre at all. I found it very untheatrical; I had been brought up to work in a traditional theatre, not just a concrete building with a theatre inside it.

After we had been playing there for a while, and I was becoming more confident about where the stage was in relation to my dressing room, I did a little exploring. I was anxious to see *The Mystery Plays*, which were on at the Cottesloe Theatre, in the same building, at the same time. Kelly Hunter, who had worked there before, and knew her way around, was in *She Stoops to Conquer* with me, and we had a very long wait between two of our scenes. One evening she came to my dressing room and said, 'Come on, Dora, let's go and have a look at *The Mystery Plays* in the Cottesloe.'

'Have·we got time?' I asked anxiously.

'Yes, we can watch half an hour of it,' replied Kelly.

In *The Mystery Plays* the audience was in the acting area with the actors. I had never been in the Cottesloe before, and didn't know what the arrangements were. I had envisaged that we could tuck ourselves away at the back, behind some seats, but not at all. There we were with the audience, in our period costumes, and getting

186

some very odd looks. I thought it was most unprofessional of Dora Bryan, the old stager, and although I had wanted so much to see *The Mystery Plays* I didn't see much of them that night because I was too worried. I felt ill at ease in my eighteenth-century costume and exaggerated wig, which made me feel hopelessly out of place and very conspicuous, and terrified in case we couldn't find our way back to the Lyttelton Theatre in time for our next entrance. When it was time to go back I just hung on to Kelly's arm, and she navigated us back to our dressing rooms in time. The trip simply wasn't worth the wear and tear on the nerves.

When a play is in rep with the National it is sometimes possible to find that there is a gap of three weeks between performances, while one of the other plays is on. This happened with *She Stoops to Conquer*, and when we returned after the break I found that all the preparation we had was a little word rehearsal, and no real on-stage rehearsal at all, which I thought frightening. One actor was so worried by this system that he went through his lines every day with his young daughter. My system was to mutter my lines quietly while walking the dogs in the park, hoping nobody would notice and think I had taken to talking to myself.

I can't help being a traditionalist about theatres, and although the National Theatre is a wonderful conception, and it is a great honour to play there, it would have been so much better if that historic theatre the Theatre Royal, Drury Lane, had been bought and used as a National Theatre. The Fortune Theatre, opposite the stage door, could have been bought as a workshop theatre, and the Strand or the Aldwych as a third. They are all in the same area, and could all have been part of the National Theatre without the expenditure of those enormous sums of money which have been lavished upon the South Bank. I cannot see why everything has to be in one vast complex, underneath all that concrete. Of course the front of the National Theatre is beautiful, facing the river as it does. It is possible to spend a whole day there without even seeing the plays. People wander in and out, browsing over the books, have a meal or a cup of tea, pop into the Film Theatre building, and there is a lovely feeling about it all. But despite all that, it's different from an old style theatre, and I don't think I could ever get used to the backstage area.

While I was in *She Stoops to Conquer* my agent telephoned to ask if I would like to do a pantomime at Brighton at the end of my National season. It sounded like a wonderful idea. A panto at Christmas within about a mile of my own home would be a real tonic after playing in a classic, and having all those train journeys to make into the bargain. Not that pantomimes are easy; they're jolly hard work, as they entail two performances a day. I realized just how hard they could be when I did *Jack and the Beanstalk* for four months at the London Palladium in 1973, with Frankie Howerd. To do just six weeks, and be able to live at home, would be sheer bliss. It would also be fun to be working in the comparatively small Theatre Royal at Brighton. My co-star in Brighton was Christopher Biggins, a great partner to work with, and a marvellous personality. He has a telephone in his dressing room, and when he's not on stage he's always on the phone to his many friends. He just loves people, and being in touch with everyone, and generally giving folks a good time. His dressing room is always more full of flowers and chocolates than that of anyone I've ever worked with, all the goodies being gifts from friends and fans. We did one number together in the pantomime, 'Diamonds are a Girl's Best Friend', dressed to the nines as Jane Russell and Marilyn Monroe, and this turned out to be a showstopper.

While doing the 1985 pantomime in Brighton I was asked to do Bernard Shaw's *The Apple Cart*, which was to open in Bath before settling down for a short run at the Haymarket Theatre. I asked Chris Biggins what he thought of the idea, and his reaction wasn't exactly encouraging. 'Oh, don't do that, Dora,' he said. 'It's such a bore!' I had played Shaw before, but *The Apple Cart* was not a play I knew, so I took down my big book of Shaw's plays from my shelf and read it through. By the time I had reached the end of it, I had to admit I thought exactly the same as Chris. But the cast list was impressive, headed by Peter O'Toole. Then there was Michael Denison, Paul Rogers, Geoffrey Keen, Marius Goring, Brewster Mason, David Waller and Bernard Braden. The ladies of the company were Dinah Sheridan, Susannah York, and Moira Lister. It was to be directed by Val May.

My role of the postmistress general was not a long one but I was on stage a lot of the time without having anything to say. This can be a bit wearing night after night, and one has to sit there looking alert and intelligent, as though one is hearing the words for the first time. During Peter O'Toole's long speech on the British monarchy, which he did magnificently, I developed the habit of popping a sweet into my mouth, praying that I wouldn't cough in the middle of his speech. I didn't, and must have appeared to be reasonably alert and intelligent, because I had some very good notices.

It was a limited run of three months at the Haymarket Theatre, so that even when we started, the end was in sight, and much as I loved the company, I was quite pleased when it finished. While I was in it, I was asked to do three musicals. My spirits rose. I just love musicals. Never a minute to become bored, and not a moment to be wasted in getting fit for the songs and the dancing. Only one of the musicals materialized, and that was *Charlie Girl*. I couldn't think why Harold Fielding wanted to revive it — apart from the fact that it had run for five and a half years at the Adelphi in 1965! It had starred Dame Anna Neagle, Joe Brown, and Derek Nimmo, and in spite of being slated by the critics, had succeeded here and in Australia. This time it was to star Cyd Charisse, that lovely American film actress and dancer. Some say she was the best partner Fred Astaire ever had. The new cast would also include Paul Nicholas, Mark Wynter, Nicholas Parsons, and me. I would have a duet with Cyd Charisse, and a lovely number 'Party of a Lifetime'.

Having complete faith in Harold Fielding and his casting director Ian Bevan, a good friend of mine, I said I would do it. I had to start rehearsals while I was still in *The Apple Cart*, and in no time at all had lost half a stone in weight, which I liked. It's much easier to dance at eight stone than at eight and a half. But the dress designer was a bit bewildered at the fittings, as the clothes had to be taken in a little more each time.

I liked Cyd Charisse on sight. A completely un-starry lady, gentle, hard-working, friendly. She has a figure I could never tire of admiring. I know the many years of dancing have helped, but she must have been a beautiful baby. Her husband, American singer Tony Martin, came over to keep her company, and he was just as nice as Cyd, proving very helpful during rehearsals with various suggestions. I missed him almost as much as Cyd did when he had to go back to the States to do some concerts. They are a devoted couple after thirty-eight years of marriage. It was wonderful to be in the show and watch this lovely lady dance every night, and I still haven't got over the fact that I was dancing with the legendary Cyd Charisse. It was a very happy show to be in. Mark Wynter is an old friend. I have done two

190

long-running pantomimes with him, a summer season, and two TV series. Paul Nicholas could charm the birds off the trees, and in *Charlie Girl* he certainly did. Nicholas Parsons is another old friend, and the whole show was like 'the party of a lifetime'.

When playing in a London show the nightly journey back to Brighton can become something of a chore, so the Victoria Palace is the ideal theatre from which to make a quick getaway to Victoria station for the Brighton train. I suppose that's why the Crazy Gang, who did so many shows at the Victoria Palace, all made their homes in Brighton. There are some compensations for making that late night journey. For me, one of them is to get back and breathe the sea air, and walk Elly, our elderly Old English sheep dog, along the quiet promenade, and know I'm safely home.

I adore all animals, and get very upset about cruelty and lack of compassion for them. I have written numerous letters in a fight against the export of live animals to Europe, as well as some protesting against factory farming. At least Mrs Thatcher replied to me. I can't say that Michael Jopling, the Minister for Agriculture, did. His department sends me a lot of gobbledygook, but it's impossible to understand.

Dogs have always been a great feature of my life. My little dog Dougal made his first appearance in pantomime at the Hippodrome, Bristol, in *Jack and the Beanstalk*. He was 'Dame Dora Doolittle's Dog Dougal'. It was explained in the script that he was 'sometimes called Fruit Gums 'cos he's always Roun'trees', and then I used to explain to the audience, 'Sometimes I call him Carpenter, 'cos when he's on the promenade that's where he does odd jobs.' (Oh dear, oh dear!) The family knew him as 'The Glenfiddich', as he was given to us in Aviemore in Scotland. He nearly died as a puppy from hardpad and distemper, but we nursed him, and fed

191

him with Brand's Essence in an eye dropper, and made certain he didn't dehydrate. Dougal's sheer determination and his inbuilt ability to survive was just one aspect of his character, and he really was a great personality with a mind of his own. In one pantomime I had a wonderful ballet scene; a send-up of *Le Spectre de la Rose*, which I originally did in *Living for Pleasure* with Terry Skelton. In the pantomime I played the Dame, and was undressing for bed, having eaten the canary for supper (a banana stuck with yellow feathers!), and when I was almost undressed, shedding the usual outrageous pantomime underwear, in through the window came dancer David Hepburn as the Spectre, dressed from head to foot in pink rose petals, and whisking me up in a passionate acrobatic dance. Unfortunately, one night Bill had failed to supervise the backstage activities of Dougal, who got out of my dressing room and found his way on to the stage. Poor David Hepburn was chased around, his tights were ruined, and his behind was nipped. Dougal thought David was attacking me, and would not let him near me. The lovely Weber music could not be heard for the cheers of the audience, who were convinced that the whole thing was rehearsed. Everyone except David Hepburn was thrilled. The theatre management congratulated us, and would have liked it kept in the show, but there was no way I could let it happen again. I liked David too much, and wanted to keep his friendship.

Dougal was responsible for putting me into many an awkward spot. He disrupted a very noisy Equity meeting at the Victoria Palace one Sunday morning. I was waiting in the wings at the side of the stage with Dougal, to get a temporary Equity card, as I'd left mine at home. Someone was making a speech, and was being heckled, whereupon Dougal rushed on stage and barked at the hecklers. It was pandemonium. He had a great sense of theatre. He once walked on stage at the Devonshire Park Theatre at Eastbourne during a quiet scene in Alan Ayckbourn's play *Relatively Speaking*. Having made his entrance he then proceeded to eat all the sugar lumps on the coffee table. Simon Williams, who was in the scene with me, loved it. We were supposed to be in a garden, and after being 'thrown' for a moment, Simon began to ad lib magnificently. 'Oh, what a dear little dog,' he said. 'What's his name?'

Me (horrified): He's not allowed in the garden.
Simon: Why not?
Me (desperate): He'll ruin the turf.
Simon (by now enjoying himself): You mean he'll cock his leg?

Dougal was having a wonderful time, basking in the limelight. He would not go offstage and stay off, but kept returning through garden doors, stage right and stage left. Anyone but Simon would quite rightly have been extremely angry. So would Alan Ayckbourn I would imagine. The ad-libbed dialogue wasn't quite up to his standard.

Despite his lapses of bad behaviour, Dougal had many redeeming features, and one was his sociability. He loved people, and it was through Dougal that I met the great Lancashire artist L.S. Lowry. I was in a play in Sunderland at the time. It was said that Lowry was attracted to the north-east because of the light in that particular area. I don't know whether that was true, but I discovered that he was staying at the same hotel as I was, which was a great thrill, because I had worshipped Lowry all my life. One day I realized he was in the hotel dining-room. I did so want to go and talk but was too nervous to approach him. Dougal wasn't a bit nervous and trotted up to the great man, wagging his tail. It was almost as though he'd said, 'Come on, Dora.

193

I'll introduce you to Mr Lowry.' The artist was so taken by this friendly little dog that the ice was broken, and I had an opportunity to meet him. I left the hotel with his autograph, which said, 'To Dora and Dougal'. The sleeve of my LP record, 'Dora Bryan Sings Five Penny Piece' featured a reproduction of a Lowry painting.

I love the story of the children at a local council school near Lowry's home in Lancashire. They wanted to buy their teacher a farewell present as she was leaving to be married. They knew she liked paintings, and one little girl said a man living in her street painted pictures. They had a collection, and raised £2. 3s. 6d. The little girl went to Lowry's house, knocked on his door, and the artist himself answered it. The little girl explained to him what she wanted and what it was for. He must have been feeling very generous, because he asked her to come back the next day, and he'd find her a suitable painting. Next day she duly knocked at the door, and Lowry came out with the painting. The little girl's face dropped. 'It isn't in a frame,' she said. 'We can't give her that.' Lowry was so amazed that he agreed to have it framed by the next day. So some lucky teacher has a Lowry painting with a delightful story attached to it.

My little dog Dougal was a great companion, and always came with me on tour. During a tour of *Relatively Speaking* we were at the King's Theatre in Southsea when there was a tremendous storm one night. Even after it had passed I couldn't sleep, so at about five o'clock in the morning I decided to take Dougal for a walk. It seemed quite a natural thing to do, and was a much more sensible way of dealing with insomnia than lying around worrying about it, so off we went. It never occurred to me that a passing policeman in a panda car would think it strange, but he slowed down slightly and gave me a curious look as he went by. Then it struck me that he must have wondered what I was doing, trotting along on my high-heeled shoes, taking a dog for a walk at that hour of the morning.

Still, it's just as well the police keep an eye on things. They have been very helpful to me at times. One night when I was appearing in Blackpool, I stayed in my dressing room after the show to watch the late night movie on TV. I suppose nobody knew I was there, and I became so engrossed in the film that time simply flew. When I finally switched off the TV set and left for home, I realized that not only had everyone else already gone, but that I had been locked in the theatre. I didn't relish spending the night there, so I looked around and found a likely looking window backstage, and climbed out. It must have been about one o'clock in the morning, and I was worried about how I was going to get back to my hotel, but — sheer magic! — I saw a taxi coming along with its light on the roof. What a relief. I hailed it and said, 'The Imperial Hotel, please.' We drove along quietly, and when we reached the hotel I got out and asked how much the fare would be. I noticed that there were two uniformed drivers, and hoped they weren't going to charge me some extortionate amount, but the reply was, 'That's all right, Miss Bryan. Have this on us. It's the police.' Friendly place, Blackpool. And how was I to know that their policemen wore caps that made them look like taxi drivers?

Dougal was with me when I was doing a Sunday night concert in Scarborough and had to get to Swansea in time to start a week's variety at the Grand Theatre. My Baptist minister friend, Frank Wilson, who was working for an organization to help drug addicts, offered to fly me from Scarborough to Swansea in a private plane. That sounded fine; a wonderful idea, so we met for breakfast at 7 a.m. on the Monday morning, and the fog was awful. A 'sea fret' they called it. We drove out to the airfield, which was really just a bumpy

195

field. To make matters worse, the previous day there had been a fatal accident. Pleasure flights and parachute jumps all took place on this airfield, and as a result of the accident the place was full of activity, with police taking measurements, which didn't do much for my confidence.

There wasn't a hope of getting off the ground until the fog had cleared. Although I had great faith in Frank, when I saw him praying in a little room in the airport building, my nerves didn't feel too good. I knew I had a band call at mid-day in Swansea, and I wished I had caught the train. But after three hours' delay we climbed into the little plane and took off, after being told to watch out for the pole at the end of the runway. So there we were — Dougal, band parts, sequins and feathers — and off we flew into the mist, just missing the pole. Frank and his co-pilot were up front. All went well until Frank announced that he would like me to look at the map for another runway. Nothing to worry about, he said, but we were getting a bit low on fuel.

We landed at Nottingham, and I wondered what all the uniformed guards were doing on the airfield, until we learnt that it was the Rolls Royce government-sponsored private airstrip, and they were very security conscious. I was sent ahead with Dougal to ask if they could let us have some fuel. The guards were neither pleased nor amused. I first of all asked for a loo, then explained about the fuel, and left Frank to deal with the rest. I reappeared from the factory, having had a coffee from a machine and given Dougal a drink from a paper cup, and was relieved to know that the plane had been re-fuelled. I paid them, and promised to do a charity show for them one day. Once more we were in the air, but then received frantic signals from the control tower to return, which we did, only to be told we had underpaid for the fuel and owed another ten pounds!

How relieved I was to arrive safely at Swansea airport. My sister-in-law, Dorothy, who lives there, and had been expecting me for hours, had drunk endless cups of tea, thinking she was never going to see me again. I missed the band call, but I'm pleased to say the opening night went very well.

So I didn't always need Dougal to get me into scrapes. I was quite good at creating my own crises, but he and I looked after each other for eight years before he died of a virus. We buried him in the garden under the peach tree, but we still have Ella, our Old English sheep dog. She loathes the limelight. We also had Maisie, who could have been Dougal's sister. Maisie now lives with our friend Jock, near Brighton race course. After two years she suddenly took a dislike to Shadow, my son William's Alsatian. Shadow has been around for eight years, and is always in and out of my home. I was afraid for Maisie, as one day she decided that Shadow couldn't come into our flat. The growling and jealousy was nerve-racking. This went on for a long time, and for Maisie's sake I had to part with her. I couldn't speak for two days without crying, but knew Jock would love her as — in his words — a little princess, and she could be the centre of attention, which some dogs need to be. She was asked to be in *She Stoops to Conquer* at the National Theatre, but I'm older and wiser now, and have enough to think about with my own performances without worrying about my dog's. Jeremy Hawk, with whom I had appeared in so many revues, once said, 'Never work with Dora Bryan or an animal. The audiences only look at them.' I think he meant it as a compliment. I've received a few back-handed ones in my time, the most recent being when I was asked to appear on a TV show with Victoria Wood. Victoria had written the sketch and described the part as 'a loud-mouthed, chain-smoking, gin-sodden old tart'. The director said, 'We must get Dora Bryan.' What is the use of my being a God-fearing teetotaller who has given up smoking?

So after fifty-two years in show business, I wonder what the best advice would be to someone just starting out? Perhaps I would have to say, 'Always be ready. You never know what you may be asked to do.' I never thought that at the age of sixty-three I'd be doing the same tap dance and splits that I did when I was twelve, and was doing so recently in *Charlie Girl*. So 'Keep fit' must be another piece of good advice. Always make certain you know your lines, and always remember that nobody is indispensable. You have to be able to take the knocks to survive. You must also be prepared to have the nearest thing to a minor heart attack each opening night. Never lose your sense of humour, and always remember that there is another world outside, so live as normal a life as possible outside the theatre. (What's normal?) Above all, look for and keep your faith in God.

The most fortunate and the most important thing in my life has been thirty-four years of being married to the best husband any actress could have. Since his retirement from cricket his life has revolved around me and our family. He is the most selfless man I know. We have had a lot of sad times in our lives, losing our babies and our parents, and coping with our son Daniel's illness, but as it has all been shared it has been easier to bear. My successes and disappointments have been his. The old proverb 'He travels fastest who travels alone' does not apply to me. I need my husband. Sometimes I have had to travel alone — to Zimbabwe, for instance, but it is a lonely life, and not for me. I would never again go so far alone, and hope that for the rest of my life I am never asked to. Although I am Dora Bryan, actress, I am equally Mrs Bill Lawton, and because I have such an understanding husband I have never been called upon to make a choice between my two roles.

Since I started these memoirs I have aged two years. They started as a scribble in a National Theatre dressing room to pass the time. They have been scribbled on trains, and in other theatre dressing rooms, and have been the cause of several burnt meals. I have gone through long periods of not writing a word, and of saying, 'It's of no interest to anyone' or 'Life is for living, not writing about.' All excuses! Why don't I admit I'm easily distracted, and can always think of other things to do? Now, I'm about to go to New York with Peter O'Toole and John Mills to play in *Pygmalion*, so perhaps this is as good a time as any to end. 'So far, so good,' as the saying goes. What's next . . .?

Whatever it is, I'll be ready.